PHOTOGRAPHY
THE AMATEUR'S GUIDE TO BETTER PICTURES

by

W9-AZP-550

HERBERT S. ZIM, Ph.D.
R. WILL BURNETT, Ph.D.
WYATT B. BRUMMITT

Illustrations and Diagrams by
HERSCHEL WARTIK
and HARRY McNAUGHT

GOLDEN PRESS

NEW YORK

FOREWORD

Photography, in just a century, has become a great medium of communication. It is a universal language, equally effective whether its task is factual or fanciful, scientific, artistic, or recreational. As an art and science it is constantly progressing. This new edition of the popular handbook that inaugurated the Golden Handbook Series combines basic principles with the latest information and developments in the field of photography.

For invaluable assistance we wish to thank many individuals and organizations, especially Mabel Priest, of the Eastman Kodak Company; Ansco; and the Polaroid Corporation. We are equally grateful to Herschel Wartik and Harry McNaught for the diagrams; to Bruce Downes and Diane Pattou, of *Popular Photography Magazine*; to Pierre Martinot and Tom Torre Bevans; and to many photographers, amateur and professional.

H.S.Z., R.W.B. and W.B.B.

Library of Congress Catalog Card Number: 64-11591
© Copyright 1964, 1956 by Golden Press, Inc. All Rights Reserved. Including the Right of Reproduction in Whole or in Part in Any Form. Designed and Produced by Artists and Writers Press, Inc. Printed in the U.S.A. by Western Printing and Lithographing Company. Published by Golden Press, Inc., New York 22, N.Y. Published simultaneously in Canada by the Musson Book Company, Ltd., Toronto
Revised Edition—First Printing, 1964

CONTENTS

Making Better Pictures

Anyone who can load a camera, point it, and click the shutter can take passably good pictures. But this book is a guide to better pictures; top-notch pictures that you can make.

This book covers all basic principles of the art and science of making better pictures. You will learn how to get the most out of your present camera, and what to look for in buying new equipment. You will learn about films and filters; how to light your subjects for different effects; how to use flash and floods; and how to make true-to-life color pictures. It will show you how to develop and print and even how to take home movies. Packed with information, this guide includes not only pointers on cameras and films but helpful suggestions on composition and the artistic and creative side of picture taking.

WHAT PICTURES? Better pictures, like better stories, are made by people who know their subject well. Your best pictures are likely to be of the things you know and value most.

Family activities Holidays are a time for capturing family fun permanently in pictures. This backyard shot of granddad and the kids getting ready for Halloween is a good example. ▶

◀ **Children** If you are willing to settle for just a good picture, take the usual snapshot of a child staring into the camera. But for shots that tell a story and are out of the ordinary, watch children at play. Wait until they've forgotten about you, and you'll get a shot like this one.

Cornelius E. Westveer—Popular Photography

Babies don't stay babies long, but you can catch their freshness and charm at each stage of their development. And if you have it on film, you and your family will have it forever. ▶

Sports ◄ Some of your best pictures of people will show action, and sports are made to order. You can catch the action of your favorite sport with an inexpensive camera and record the thrills of the game. Take your camera along.

Milestones such as new babies, birthdays, Johnny's first suit, and Mary's wedding day should be captured on film. Make them informal. ►

Phoebe Dunn

School days ◄ are sources of better pictures. Shots like this need no words to help tell their story. Use your camera to capture the campus mood or to record your impressions of buildings, games, friends, and events—the familiar things you want to remember.

Underwood & Underwood

6

▲ **Travel**   Take your camera along on trips to record the beauty you see and the fun you have. Learn to see the story your subjects have to tell. For example, mountain lakes, which have been pictured thousands of times, can still challenge you with their moods of majesty, mystery, power, and beauty. Can you capture them on your film?

Nature   A really good picture requires a seeing eye. So your first and hardest task in taking better pictures is to learn to see the line, form, color, and beauty of everyday things around you. One of your best subjects is Mother Nature. Look at this picture of a cactus in bloom; it emphasizes the contrast between the flower's delicacy and the stalk's spiky sternness. The result is a much better picture.   ▶

THE RIGHT START The best way to start taking better pictures is to learn a few simple rules that apply to any kind of camera. Once you get the feel of your camera and can size up your subject so you get good pictures nine times out of ten, you are ready to start making better pictures. What you need most is experience. Take pictures based on the rules on the next four pages.

Keep a record of what you do and refer to it as you study the pictures. Learn from your mistakes as well as your successes. After each shot, jot down facts about the subject, time of day, sun or shade, and distance to camera. When you get your prints back, study each picture. Check against the data you have jotted down.

On the next page is a seven-point starter of basic rules. Follow them closely at first, especially if you're a beginner. With a simple box camera, just start shooting. If your camera has adjustable features, set the focus at 15 ft., the diaphragm at f/16, and the shutter speed at 1/50 sec. This way, your camera is set much like a box camera. It will work fine for average conditions with ordinary, medium-speed film, and you'll learn the basic facts of picture taking faster if you don't worry about all sorts of camera settings. So load your camera and start!

Subject does not face directly into sun

No closer than 6 ft.

Sun behind you

Hold camera steady

KEEP THESE RULES IN MIND

1 **Be sure your camera is loaded.** You'd be surprised at how often even experts lose beautiful shots because they forget to put film in their cameras.

2 **Advance your film after each shot.** Double exposures may give an interesting effect, but it's usually one that you don't want.

3 **Hold your camera steady, or place it on a firm support.** Hold it steady, hold your breath, and squeeze the button slowly. More pictures have been ruined by unsteady cameras than by any other single cause.

4 **Keep your distance—not closer than 6 ft.** Most box cameras or a camera with box-camera lens settings can't focus closer than 6 ft. without an auxiliary lens. So keep your distance for sharp focus.

5 **Catch your subject when it isn't moving.** A shutter speed of 1/50 sec. won't stop motion unless your subject is pretty far away. The closer the subject is, the less motion you can tolerate. *But*—you don't have to ask a person to freeze. Don't count or give warning. Watch for that moment when your subject is poised motionless —then squeeze the button.

6 **Shoot with the sun behind you.** Light paints the picture in photography. In open sunlight let the light fall on your subject, not on your camera. Let the sun shine from behind you over your shoulder. But don't make your subject squint directly into the sun—no one can look natural that way.

7 **For better portraits, shoot in open shade.** Open sunlight makes harsh shadows. For the best pictures of people try shooting in open shade—as in the shade at the north side of a house, bright sky overhead.

1. Have a subject.

2. Tell a story.

3. Work for unity.

4. Emphasize your point.

PICTURE LANGUAGE People take pictures to tell others what they see and feel. Years of experience have produced some basic ideas on how best to tell these things through pictures:

1 A good picture has a subject—a reason for being. If the viewer has to hunt for the subject, the picture is a poor one. So, before you shoot, be sure you know why you're taking the picture.

2 A better picture always has a point—a story to tell. Be sure your subject is so placed and your camera angle so set that the story will come through.

3 A better picture has unity. It is complete in both idea and presentation. You feel that everything necessary to the story is there and properly emphasized.

4 A better picture draws the eye to the thing you want emphasized. Your subject stands out. This, too, is a matter of arrangement, camera angle, and background.

From these principles come a number of practical hints (pp. 54-55) to help you take better pictures. Follow these rules, but don't be a slave to them.

8

Light and Your Camera

You've been taking pictures right along, of course. If you have followed the basic rules in the preceding pages, you have probably taken some good ones. But you want better pictures. Getting them requires a knowledge of light and how to control it. From the pressing of the button to the final processing of the print, it is light that controls the picture in photography. To get better pictures, you must learn how to get the light just where you want it.

First, you need to understand how light makes your pictures and how to use your camera for better light control. Later, this book will help you to learn how to control light for better color pictures (pp. 41-52) and how to use light in the darkroom to get the most out of your negatives (pp. 124-125). Start experimenting as you take pictures. Try all sorts of shots based on the material in this section. Be creative—experiment. And don't forget to record what you do. Learn from your finished prints so that each picture you take will be better than the one before it.

A light flash of 1/5000 sec. stops a bird on the wing.

Walker Van Ripper—Denver Mus. of Nat. Hist.

A 94-min. exposure accumulates faint light from distant stars.

sunlight (white light)   **prism**

LIGHT is a stream of tiny particles called "photons" which radiate from any light source at the incredible speed of 186,000 miles per sec. Photons move in a perfectly straight path unless something gets in their way. When the stream hits something—and this is what is important in photography—it may be reflected, absorbed, diffused, or bent.

1 Most surfaces reflect some light. If the surface is mirror-smooth, the photons bounce off, or are reflected, in a regular pattern. But light reflected from an irregular surface—a book, a house, or a person's body—is reflected irregularly. Such light, reflected from our subjects, enters our camera and makes our pictures.

2 Most surfaces absorb some light. Dark-colored objects absorb more light than light-colored objects. Such differences in light absorption and reflection cause the contrasts in what we see. But your eyes can see far more shades of contrast than the best films can, and this fact

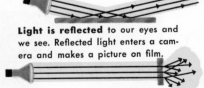

Light is reflected to our eyes and we see. Reflected light enters a camera and makes a picture on film.

Light is diffused, or scattered, when passing through clouds or frosted glass. It forms soft shadows.

Light is also absorbed. Red objects absorb all but red light, green all but green light of the solar spectrum.

Solar spectrum appears when sunlight is broken up by prism (see p. 32).

creates a problem in photography. To get detail in both the lightest and the darkest parts of one picture requires skill and experience.

3 Light is diffused when it passes through some materials; it is scattered in all directions. Diffused light is softer and forms soft shadows. That is why your best outdoor portraits will usually be made on overcast days when sunlight is diffused through the clouds. (Irregularly reflected light is much like diffused light.)

4 Light is bent when it goes through a transparent material such as water or glass. A straight stick looks bent when placed in a glass of water. A camera lens, thicker in the middle than at the edges, bends the light to form an image of the object on the film.

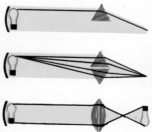

Light is bent when it passes through curved or wedge-shaped glass. Special prisms and lenses bend light without separating colors of white light. Light is always bent toward thickest part of glass. Two prisms placed with bases together will bend light as shown in middle picture. A convex lens will bend light to form an image as shown in bottom picture.

13

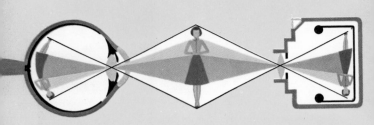

Your eyes and your camera are in some ways alike. Light is bent by the lens and forms an upside-down image at the back of each.

PHOTOGRAPHS ARE LIGHT PICTURES
As you read this page, light enters your eyes and excites the nerves which are sensitive to it. When you take a picture, light enters the camera and changes the silver chemicals which coat the film. In a way, your eye and a camera work alike; and with cameras and films you can take a picture of almost anything you can see. Sometimes you can photograph things you can't see (p. 143).

But there are big differences between seeing an object clearly and getting a sharp photograph of it. Your eyes continuously and automatically adjust to differences in light. Your eyes focus automatically, regardless of how far away an object is. Your eyes focus without your thinking about it. But the eye (or lens) of a camera does not adjust automatically for differences in light intensity and distance. You have to think for your camera if you want clear, sharp photographs. Box cameras are set for average conditions. Even with such cameras, some knowledge of light control and judgment born of experience improve results greatly. Light makes the picture in every photograph. Learn to control light and you will get better pictures.

HOW LIGHT MAKES THE PICTURE

When you press the button, a shutter opens and light streams into the camera for a fraction of a second. A glass lens bends the light and causes it to fall on the film, forming the image which becomes your picture.

When you click the shutter . . .

Wherever that light hits, a change takes place in the light-sensitive silver chemicals with which the film is coated. An invisible, or latent, image is thus formed. You can't see it, but you've got your picture!

. . . an invisible image forms on the film.

When the film is placed in a developing solution, the latent image becomes visible, but everything is reversed—black is white and white is black. That is why the developed film is called a negative.

Developing brings out visible negative image.

Next, a printing paper covered with similar light-sensitive silver chemicals is exposed to light sent through the negative. The image that appears on the paper is reversed again, so that white is white and black is black, truly representing your original scene. This is your final picture or print.

If you controlled the light correctly, your picture will be clear.

Printing reverses blacks and whites of negative.

LOOK AT A CAMERA   A camera is essentially a light-tight box (1) with an opening to allow a controlled amount of light to enter and strike the film, held in focal-plane position by film-advance system (2). Every camera has a shutter (5) —a door which opens momentarily to admit light. Except in the simplest cameras, you can make precise changes in the amount of time the shutter is open. The lens (3) bends the light to form the image on the film. With most cameras you can adjust the lens with a

INSIDE A CAMERA

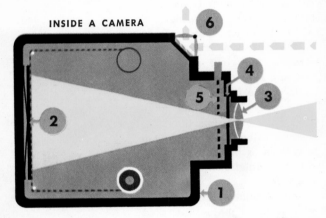

device that moves it forward or back according to whether the object is near or far away. If this adjustment, or focus, is inaccurate, the light image—and the picture it makes—will be blurred. The lenses of box cameras are set for reasonably sharp focus from about 6 ft. away to any distance beyond. The focus of such lenses cannot be changed. Most kinds of cameras have a diaphragm (4) which can be regulated to admit varying amounts of light while the shutter is open. And all cameras have some kind of viewer (6) so that you can see accurately what you are photographing. Details on pages 90-101.

1 light-proof box

ESSENTIAL PARTS OF A CAMERA

Light-proof box Regardless of shape and size, the camera body must keep out all light except that coming through the lens when the shutter is open.

2 film advancer

Film advancer A mechanism for advancing the film. It is connected to a device which keeps the film flat and in position for light image to hit it properly.

3 lens

Lens Lenses vary in size, shape, and construction, but all have one function—to bend light so it will form a sharp image on the film when the shutter opens.

4 diaphragm

Diaphragm The diaphragm is like the iris of the eye and serves the same function—to admit an exact amount of light each moment the shutter is open.

5 shutter

Shutter Some are made of tiny, movable fins of metal and are placed in the lens mounting. Others are like a window shade with slits in it and are placed in the camera back. All are designed to open and close in a precise amount of time.

6 viewer

Viewer Some are of ground glass, some are simple windows. Some have their own lenses, some are wire frames and use no lenses. All are designed to help you see what picture you will get.

BRIGHT SUNLIGHT

Shadows strong, sharp contrasts between blacks and whites

CLOUDS DIFFUSE LIGHT

Shadows light, soft gradations between blacks and whites

LIGHT AND SHADOW The basic problem in photography is to have your camera record the most desirable pattern of light and shadow. With ordinary black-and-white film, different colors are rendered in terms of black, white, and many shades of gray. Gradations from black to white give shape, texture, and feeling to the subject. For most pictures you will want a normal contrast between the blacks and whites, with many gradations in between. Too much contrast, as in an overexposed beach scene, means loss of detail. Sometimes, however, you will want a hard picture, in which the blacks and

A picture with very little contrast has many shades of gray and little pure black and white. It is particularly effective here.

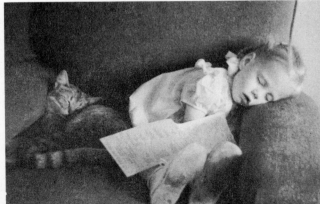

Normal contrast—balanced detail

Overexposed—unbalanced detail

whites are in sharp contrast, with few grays and little detail. Such pictures suggest ruggedness, strength, and power. Contrast is frequently used for dramatic impact. Occasionally a soft picture of very little contrast is desired to carry the feeling of gentleness, tranquillity, and serenity. This softness is often used for feminine portraits or to give special effects to scenic views. Control of contrast, therefore, is of great importance in your finished picture. It can be controlled by three things—lighting (pp. 20-21), exposure (pp. 38-40), and development of the film and prints (pp. 108-115).

Pictures in sharp contrast are useful for dramatic impact.

Leon Levinstein—Popular Photography

LIGHTING YOUR SUBJECT   The safest plan for outdoor portraits in black and white is to place your subject in open shade. This produces normal contrast.

Over-shoulder lighting   For outdoor portraits in direct sunlight, the simplest plan is to have the sun illuminate your subject from over your shoulder. This gives side shadow for depth. Your picture will have more contrast, but with proper exposure it will be sharp.

Side lighting   When the sun illuminates your subject from full right or left, one side is fully lighted and the other is in deep shadow. The contrast will usually be too strong for portraits unless some kind of reflector is used to lighten the shadowed side. The reflector can be the side of a house, a large piece of white cardboard, or any other reflecting surface placed 2 or 3 ft. from the shadow side of your subject. Sometimes strong side shadows are desirable for dramatic effect.

Front lighting   If the sun is directly behind you and lights your subject head-on, you will lose most of the shadows; your picture will lack detail and may look flat. Front-lighted portraits may show great contrast between the brightly-lighted areas and the shadowed ones, but the subject's face will seem flat and chalky, with harsh vertical shadows cast by the brows, nose, and lips. Front lighting is seldom useful for portraits, pictures of houses, or other single subjects.

Back lighting   If the sun comes from behind your subject, it forms a silhouette—a dark form without detail. Ordinarily you would avoid such lighting. But back-lighted pictures can be the most exciting ones you take. Use back lighting for interesting moods, dramatic effects. CAUTION: With back lighting, always screen your lens from direct sunlight with a lens shade or cardboard, or you'll get glares of light that spoil your picture.

Over-shoulder lighting
is generally the best.

Side lighting gives
harsh shadows.

Front lighting loses shadows
and hence detail.

Back lighting produces
silhouette effect.

21

Wide opening throws bright image on film.

Narrow opening admits less light to film.

LIGHT CONTROL
Exposure is the total amount of light reaching the film. Depending on the amount of light available, lens and shutter, balanced one against the other, give the right exposure for your picture.

Lens opening Light entering the camera passes through an opening called the "aperture." Most box cameras have a single, fixed aperture. Most other cameras have a diaphragm, used to make the aperture larger or smaller. The larger the aperture, the greater the amount of light that enters the camera during a given moment.

Shutter Speed The amount of light that reaches the film depends also upon how long the shutter is open. The slower the shutter speed, the more light enters. Most box cameras have fixed shutter speeds—about 1/50 sec. The pictures below demonstrate equivalent but different exposures. On the left the picture was taken with a shutter speed of 1/50 sec. at f/22; on the right, 1/200 sec. at f/11 stopped the white car which was moving.

Small opening, slow shutter

Wide opening, fast shutter

DEPTH OF FIELD Nearly every picture subject has depth. Parts of the subject are nearer the camera than other parts are. To have front and back elements equally distinct, your lens must focus sharply through the whole depth of the group as in Picture 1. This was taken with a box camera of the fixed-focus type. Everything beyond about 5½ ft. is fairly sharp. The same results can be obtained with other cameras by closing down the lens aperture.

Picture 2 was also taken with a box camera with a fixed-focus. The girl was too near the camera and is out of focus. Sometimes this effect is desired and can be achieved with other cameras by focusing on rear objects with a wide-open aperture.

Picture 3 was taken with an adjustable-focus camera. The girl, 4 ft. from the camera, is in sharp focus, while the man and background are out of focus. Thus attention is directed to the girl. The total background is soft and does not distract.

Depth of field is always most difficult to obtain when at close range. It can be increased by cutting down the size of the aperture. Close the diaphragm down. Slow down the shutter speed so that the light admitted remains the same as before. Focus about one third of the way between the nearest and farthest subject. Your picture will be like Picture 1.

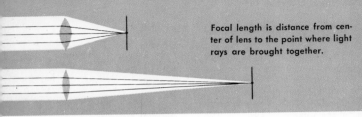

Focal length is distance from center of lens to the point where light rays are brought together.

LENSES AND "F" NUMBERS

When parallel light rays go through the lens of a camera, they are brought together or focus at some point behind the lens. The distance from the center of the lens to this point is called the "focal length." This is determined by the shape of the lens and it never changes.

A second unchanging characteristic of any lens is its f number. This is the ratio between the diameter of the lens and its focal length. The number indicates what fraction the diameter is of that focal length. For example, an f/4 lens has a diameter ¼ of its focal length, and an f/2 lens has a diameter ½ of its focal length. As the diameter of an f/2 lens is twice that of an f/4 lens of the same focal length, its area is four times as great. It admits four times as much light—it is four times as fast as the f/4 lens.

Cameras with diaphragms have f numbers marked. Numbers most used are: 2, 2.8, 4, 5.6, 8, 11, 16, 22—the major stops. Intermediate stops include 3.5, 4.5, and 6.3.

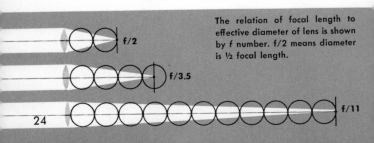

The relation of focal length to effective diameter of lens is shown by f number. f/2 means diameter is ½ focal length.

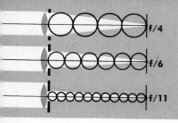

Cutting down size of aperture with a diaphragm effectively changes the *f* number of a lens.

The range varies with each camera type. One may start with f/4 and close down to f/16. Another may go from f/2.8 to f/22. Remember that f numbers are fractions. The larger the number, the smaller the fraction of light reaching the film. Closing the diaphragm from one major stop to the next cuts light reaching the film by one-half; from a major to an intermediate stop, by about one-fourth.

Speed and lens opening are complementary. Each combination of diaphragm settings and shutter speeds charted below will admit the same amount of light. So a setting of 1/50 sec. at f/8 gives exactly the same exposure as any of the other combinations shown. The best combination to use depends on depth of field desired and motion of your subject.

Some of the modern cameras vary lens opening automatically as light changes (pp. 38-39), so exposure stays both correct and constant for any shutter speed that you may choose.

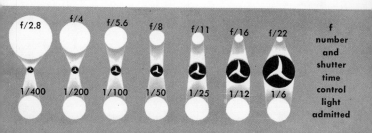

f/2.8	f/4	f/5.6	f/8	f/11	f/16	f/22	f number and shutter time control light admitted
1/400	1/200	1/100	1/50	1/25	1/12	1/6	

KEEPING IN FOCUS   A beginner may find that a box camera gives him better pictures than a more complicated one. A box camera has a pre-set focus and will take any subject over 6 ft. away with average sharpness. An expensive camera must be properly focused, but will take sharper pictures than the box camera can. But no camera can focus sharply on all distances at once.

The job is made easier by cutting down the aperture The smaller this is, the greater is the depth of the field in which everything is in clear focus. See table below. Notice that stopping down the diaphragm increases sharpness of focus faster beyond the place of exact focus than nearer to the camera. For close-ups, use smallest aperture possible with the available light.

Greatest depth of field results from small aperture and focusing about one-third of the way from nearest to farthest object you want clear. Note picture at bottom left, p.27. Focus was on no. 6 ball at f/22. All is fairly distinct. In second picture, focus was on 6 ball but aper-

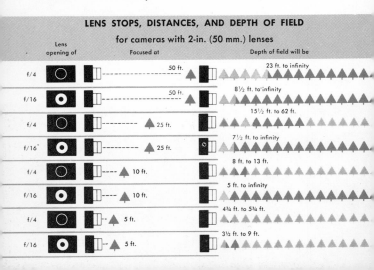

LENS STOPS, DISTANCES, AND DEPTH OF FIELD
for cameras with 2-in. (50 mm.) lenses

Lens opening of		Focused at	Depth of field will be
f/4		50 ft.	23 ft. to infinity
f/16		50 ft.	8½ ft. to infinity
f/4		25 ft.	15½ ft. to 62 ft.
f/16		25 ft.	7½ ft. to infinity
f/4		10 ft.	8 ft. to 13 ft.
f/16		10 ft.	5 ft. to infinity
f/4		5 ft.	4¾ ft. to 5¾ ft.
f/16		5 ft.	3½ ft. to 9 ft.

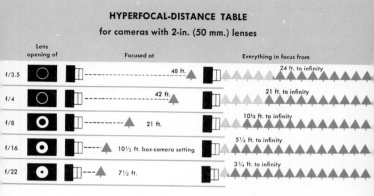

HYPERFOCAL-DISTANCE TABLE

for cameras with 2-in. (50 mm.) lenses

Lens opening of			Focused at	Everything in focus from
f/3.5			48 ft.	24 ft. to infinity
f/4			42 ft.	21 ft. to infinity
f/8			21 ft.	10½ ft. to infinity
f/16			10½ ft. box-camera setting	5¼ ft. to infinity
f/22			7½ ft.	3¾ ft. to infinity

ture was opened to f/5.6. Fewer balls are distinct. Fewer still are clear in third picture taken also at f/5.6 but with focus on no. 1 ball.

Some cameras have a depth-of-field scale. The table above gives the same information. For a given lens and stop, focusing at hyperfocal distance brings everything from half that distance to infinity into focus. For example, to get pictures without changing focus, set your lens at f/8, focus at 21 ft. (hyperfocal distance), and everything from 10½ ft. to infinity will be sharp. Many cameras have the 50 mm. lens used in this table.

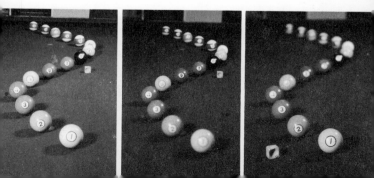

ACTION SHOTS Posed pictures have their place, but it is the unposed ones that can be really exciting. Pictures showing action are not difficult to take if you understand two things about motion:

Distance from camera The farther away a subject is from the camera, the slower its speed seems. An airplane traveling 200 miles an hour appears almost motionless when very far away.

Direction of motion A train speeding away from you at 60 miles an hour gets small rapidly, but it is easier to stop with your camera than a train going past you at the same speed.

The table below takes these factors into account and gives examples to help you judge the shutter speed you will need to stop most motion.

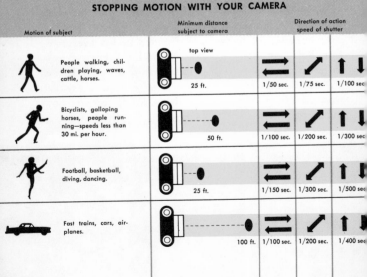

STOPPING MOTION WITH YOUR CAMERA

Motion of subject		Minimum distance subject to camera	Direction of action speed of shutter		
	People walking, children playing, waves, cattle, horses.	top view 25 ft.	⇄ 1/50 sec.	↗ 1/75 sec.	↑↓ 1/100 sec
	Bicyclists, galloping horses, people running—speeds less than 30 mi. per hour.	50 ft.	⇄ 1/100 sec.	↗ 1/200 sec.	↑↓ 1/300 sec
	Football, basketball, diving, dancing.	25 ft.	⇄ 1/150 sec.	↗ 1/300 sec.	↑↓ 1/500 sec
	Fast trains, cars, airplanes.	100 ft.	⇄ 1/100 sec.	↗ 1/200 sec.	↑↓ 1/400 sec

◄ Not fast-action shot, but a poised-action shot taken when action stopped at the top of roller coaster's arc.

Another poised action shot. Pole vaulter caught at peak of climb on Ektachrome Film at 1/200 sec. and f/3.5. ▼

R. L. Propst—Popular Photography

MOTION - STOPPING TRICKS

Top-flight action shots often depend more on timing than on shutter speed. Shooting at just the instant when the action is suspended—when there is a stopping point or pause—is one of the best tricks. A diver at the top of his spring, a pitcher all wound up ready to throw—such shots do not need super-speed shutters. Get your focus, aperture, and shutter settings ready ahead of time and shoot at the precise second action pauses in a poised position.

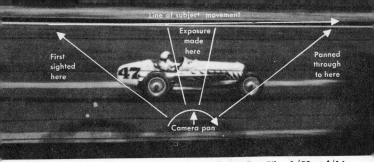

Line of subject movement

First sighted here

Exposure made here

Panned through to here

Camera pan

Panning stopped this racer. Kodak Verichrome Pan Film, 1/50 at f/16.

PANNING Even a box camera with a shutter speed of about 1/50 sec. can produce beautiful shots of speeding cars or planes by the method called "panning." You pivot or swing the camera smoothly to keep it lined up on the passing action and trip the shutter in the middle of the swing. Don't stop, don't pause. Swing, snap, and follow-through. Fore and background may be blurred, but the moving object will be quite sharp if you've panned smoothly and at the right speed. Try it a few times with an empty camera before you take a real shot.

Panned shot on Kodak Tri-X Film, 1/100 at f/16. Note blurred background.

This mallard was caught on Koda-chrome Daylight Film, 1/250 at f/4. Note effect of blurred, fast-moving wing tips. ▶

BLUR GIVES FEELING OF SPEED If you pan too rapidly or too slowly, your subject will be blurred as well as the background. Sometimes such blurriness is

desirable to give the sensation of motion and speed to your picture. Try it in some action shots. Take several shots, panning more rapidly each time, and compare the results. Notice how a little blur adds to the feeling of speed. Too much blur conveys the impression of high speed but your subject may lose form entirely. Try a slow shutter on a dance shot for blur. You'll find it may add greatly to the feeling of graceful motion. A slow shutter will blur feet and hands of walking persons, giving impression of motion with clear detail of face and body.

Slow panning blurs cyclists, giving effect of speed.

Films, Light, and Exposure

Your film is basically a thin sheet of plastic coated with an emulsion of gelatin containing microscopic grains of a light-sensitive silver chemical. This sensitivity varies with the size of the silver grains and other film properties. Some films are fast: they react to dim light or to very short exposure. Slow, fine-grain films, in general, give a negative more sharpness. Some films like Kodak's Tri-X combine extreme speed with fair sharpness.

The speed of films is standardized on an "ASA" scale that runs from 1 to 800 or more. The higher the number, the faster the film. A film with an index number of 80 is twice as fast as a 40. Values differ for sunlight and for artificial (tungsten) light. Most film comes in rolls, but some cameras use film packs, cut film, or glass plates.

LIGHT, passed through a prism, breaks up into its component colors, or spectrum. Black-and-white films differ in their sensitivity to different parts of the spectrum. Panchromatic (pan) films, sensitive to all visible spectrum colors, give pictures a natural range of tones. Orthochromatic (ortho) films are sensitive to blue and green but almost blind to red light. Not generally available to amateurs, ortho film is used by professionals for contrast effects.

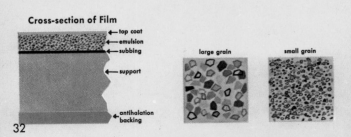

Cross-section of Film
← top coat
← emulsion
← subbing
← support
← antihalation backing

large grain   small grain

FILM SPEEDS OF SOME COMMONLY USED BLACK-AND-WHITE FILMS

NAME		INDEX (New ASA)		CHARACTERISTICS
		Day.	Tung.	
Adox				
35 mm.	120 Roll			
KB14	R14	20	16	Ultra-fine grain, slow.
KB17	R17	40	32	Fine grain, moderate speed.
KB21	R21	100	80	Fine grain, fast.
Agfa				
Isopan-IFF		25	25	Ultra-fine grain, slow. 35 mm. and roll.
Isopan-IF		80	80	Very fine grain, moderate speed. 35 mm. and roll.
Isopan-ISS		200	200	Moderate grain, fast. 35 mm. and roll.
Isopan-Ultra (All in 35 mm. and roll)		400	400	Moderate grain, very fast, for dim light and fast motion photography. 35 mm. and roll.
Ansco				
Super Hypan (35 mm. and roll)		500		Extreme speed; moderate grain. General purpose as well as for dim light and motion.
All-Weather Pan (Roll film only)		125	50	Outdoor and flash especially.
FR Subminiature (for 16 mm. Minolta Cameras)				(Kodachrome and Anscochrome also available for Minoltas)
Panatomic-X		40	40	Extreme fine grain, sharpness.
Plus-X		160	125	Fine grain, fast, general purpose.
Tri-X		400	320	Extreme speed; moderate grain for dim light, and fast motion.
Kodak				
Panatomic-X		40	40	Extreme fine grain, moderate speed, sharp.
Plus-X		160	125	Fine grain, fast, general purpose.
Tri-X		400	320	Extreme speed, moderate grain.
Verichrome Pan		125	125	
(All but Verichrome in 35 mm. and rolls. Verichrome in rolls only.)				

Sensitivity of the eye

Panchromatic film

Orthochromatic film

NAME   INDEX   CHARACTERISTICS

Color Film for Projection Slides (color prints can be made)

Agfa

Agfachrome	50	35 mm. and 120, 127 rolls. Daylight, blue flash-bulbs and electronic flash.

Ansco

Anscochrome 50	50	Fast. Daylight only. 35 mm. only.
Anscochrome 100	100	Very fast. Daylight or tungsten. 35 mm. only.
Anscochrome 200	200	Fastest color film made. Daylight only. (Use filters for artificial light.) 35 mm. only.

Kodak

Kodachrome II	25	Excellent color rendition. 35 mm. and 828 roll. Daylight and tungsten types.
Kodachrome-X	64	Less sharpness, more contrast, and darker reds than Kodachrome II but excellent for fast action or poor light conditions. 35 mm. and 126 roll.
Ektachrome-X	64	35 mm. and most roll sizes. Daylight, blue flashbulbs, and electronic flash. Rich reds and sharp yellows. Home processing possible.
High Speed Ektachrome type B	125	Extreme speed for artificial lighting only. For night street scenes, interiors, shows. 35 mm. only.
High Speed Ektachrome	160	Extreme speed with consequent loss in sharpness. But marvelous for action-stopping. Daylight only. 35 mm. only.

Color Film for Color Prints

Agfa

Agfacolor CN17	40	Reasonably fast and sharp. 35 mm. and 120, 620 rolls.

Kodak

Kodacolor-X	64	Fast and reasonably sharp. 35 mm. and 126 rolls. Home processing possible.

(See p. 33 for 16 mm. color films under FR subminiature)

WHICH FILM TO USE

For sharp enlargements use a fine-grain film—ultra-fine for over-size enlargements. If light is dim, you are forced to high-speed film. For all around use, a medium-speed film (40 to 80) is generally best. Experiment with very fast film such as Tri-X or Super Hypan for night scenes with ordinary artificial light.

Color Films differ in speed and color rendition. None is perfect. Experiment for transparencies you like best.

Without Polaroid polarizing filter   With Polaroid polarizing filter

FILTERS for black-and-white photography. After you've photographed landscapes and found the clouds missing in the prints, you'll start using filters. A filter is a colored disc through which some colors cannot pass. It fits over your camera lens and corrects for limited film sensitivity.

You can use any of over a hundred kinds of filters. Four have wide use: yellow (Wratten K2); orange (Wratten G); red (Wratten A); and green Wratten X1). Their uses are shown on the next two pages. Be sure to get filters that fit your lens, as they are made in various sizes.

Most filters cut down on light entering the camera. When using such filters, increase the exposure. The filter factor, or number of times the exposure must be increased, varies with the filter used. For a factor of 2, cut your speed in half, or open your diaphragm to the next major stop. Don't use these filters for color film.

Color film filters are also made. Some cut haze and are helpful in long-view scenics, some polarize light and eliminate unwanted reflections, and others permit you to use a daylight color film by artificial light.

Polaroid polarizing filters cut down glare from surfaces such as glass, water, and polished wood. They are useful for shooting through window glass. The Neutral Polaroid filter has a factor of 2.5 in daylight or artificial light.

FILTER USES

Wratten K2 for natural-looking skies, smooth skin texture, and natural textures in sunlit buildings, wood, and fabrics.

Wratten X1 for the most natural reproduction of multicolored subjects such as flowers pictured against green foliage. Flowers stand out in bold relief. Use also for portraits shot against the sky.

Wratten A for spectacular, stormy-looking skies; to cut through haze for long-distance shots and shots from the air; for brilliant sunsets; for greater detail of red, orange, and bronze-colored flowers.

Wratten G for darkened skies, haze penetration, increased texture of stone, wood, brick, and fabrics, and for marine scenes.

FILTER FACTORS

Wratten K2, clear yellow, brought city and clouds into better relief. Filter factors — Panchromatic: sun, 2; flash, 1.5.

with filter

Wratten X1, green, made these flowers come to life. Filter factors — Panchromatic: sun, 4; flash, 3.

with filter

Wratten A, red, gave a dramatic quality to these clouds. Filter factors — Panchromatic: sun, 8; flash, 4

with filter

Wratten G, orange, emphasized water and sky. Filter factors—Panchromatic: sun, 3; flash, 2.

◀ **Reflected-light meters** Point meter at subject.

Incident meters Hold near subject; point at camera. ▶

EXPOSURES The right exposure for any shot is, simply, the combination of shutter speed and aperture which will, under existing conditions, get the right amount of light to the film. First of these conditions is, of course, the light available. Second is the sensitivity of the film you are using. Third is the shutter speed needed to stop the action involved. Fourth is the lens aperture you need for the depth of field. All of these will seldom be ideal. You will have to compromise on one to get another. But to do so intelligently—to make the best exposure for the story you want your picture to tell—takes judgment; and judgment comes only from experience. So experiment. Keep a record of your exposures and the conditions under which you made them so that you can learn.

To make accurate exposures, you must learn to estimate exposure requirements accurately. There are many devices, calculators, and meters to help you. The handiest are the printed calculators, such as the ASA Computer

GE PR-1

Kodak Automatic 35F with built-in exposure meter

Weston Master II

and the Kodaguides. Start
with whichever of the three
factors is most important to
you — light, speed, or aperture. The dial gives an estimate of the other two factors.

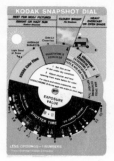

Kodak Snapshot Dial

Photoelectric meters remove
the guesswork. They contain
cells which react to light by
producing tiny but measur-
able electric currents. The
greater the light, the stronger
the current which moves a pointer on a calibrated dial.
Pointer setting gives scale position from which you can
select from combinations of apertures and shutter speeds
(all providing the same exposure). Which combination
you use depends on several factors (see table below).
Some meters are for use from the camera position, and
react to light reflected from the subject. Others (incident
meters) register the light falling on your subject.

Many cameras have built-in light meters. Some do all
the figuring. Set the diaphragm and the meter keeps exposure constant by automatically changing shutter speed,
or set the speed and the f stops change automatically.

Your calculator or meter may tell you to use any combination of these apertures
and shutter speeds shown below.

Apertures . . .	2.8	3.5	4	4.5	5.6	8	11	16	22
and Shutter Speeds	1/800	1/500	1/400	1/300	1/200	1/100	1/50	1/25	1/10

Which to use depends on which of the factors below are most important.

Stopping Motion	very sharply stopped	sharply stopped	slightly blurred	blurred
Depth of Field	very shallow	shallow	medium	deep	very deep
Focusing Problem	increasingly great because of decreasing depth of field	less great, because of depth of field		

Beach and snow

Open landscape

Street scene

BASIC OUTDOOR EXPOSURE CHART

The chart below will help you estimate exposures accurately without meters. It assumes a film speed of 50 to 80 and 1/50 sec. shutter speed—both average.

Basic Outdoor Exposure Chart			
bright sunlight	hazy	cloudy	dull
f/16	11	8	5.6
f/11	8	5.6	4
f/8	5.6	4	2.8

Use this chart as a basic guide; also experiment. The table calls for f/11 at 1/50 sec. for photographing a building in bright sunlight. If it is a dark building, try opening the aperture a stop or two; if a light building, halfway between f/11 and f/16 might be best.

Louis Stettner—Popular Photography

Pictures in Color

Modern color films can capture the rainbow. They can record the most vibrant and the most delicate of colors. And with flood or flash equipment (pp. 78-89) you can take color shots around the clock.

Color photography used to be only for the skilled experimenter. Now, thanks to modern films and processing techniques, anyone who can take good black-and-white pictures can take good color pictures. The same basic rules of exposure and composition hold.

There are some differences, such as problems of lighting (the color of sunlight at noon is very different from its color at sunset). There are also problems of reflected light never encountered with black-and-white film because the sensitive film picks up reflected colors your eyes see but hardly notice. But color work opens up new horizons for the amateur.

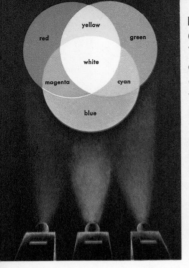

Red, green, and blue light combine to produce white light and other colors.

HOW COLOR WORKS

Color is light—light is color. White light has in it all the colors of the spectrum, but any of them can be reproduced with mixtures of three colors—red, green, and blue. When those three colors of light are of equal strength, white light is the result; but control and vary the amount of red, blue, or green light, and you can get almost any color. Color photography breaks up the colors of a scene into the three basic colors and records them on film in their proper proportions. To do this, Kodachrome and similar color films are made of three separate emulsions and one filter. The top emulsion is sensitive only to blue light; the second to green and blue; the third to red and blue. A yellow filter between the top two layers prevents blue light from going beyond the blue-sensitive layer.

Each color in the original scene affects one or more layers of the film. A green dress, for example, affects only the middle layer. Development, a reversal process, dyes the layers not affected by the original light. The film area affected by the green dress, for example, is dyed yellow in the top layer and blue in the bottom layer. The middle (green-sensitive) layer is not affected by the dyes and becomes transparent. But when white light is projected through that section of the film, the yellow and blue dyes act like filters, producing the original green color of the dress on the screen.

Color transparency films   Home movies, color slides, and some commercial forms of color photographs are transparencies. Light passes through them to give you the color result; it may be light in a projector or the light against which you look at the picture. From transparencies there are various ways to produce color prints.

Negative color films   The most popular snapshot color film is one which produces a color negative, from which positive color prints and enlargements are then made. In the color negative, the colors you see are complementary to the actual colors of the scene. So it is just as truly a negative as is a black-and-white negative.

While color printing is still nothing for beginners to bother with, there is real hope that soon (assuming you have really mastered black-and-white darkroom techniques, including enlarging) you may be able to make color enlargements with your own equipment. And you will be able to control things all the way, just as with black-and-white film.

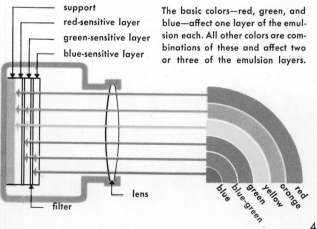

support
red-sensitive layer
green-sensitive layer
blue-sensitive layer

The basic colors—red, green, and blue—affect one layer of the emulsion each. All other colors are combinations of these and affect two or three of the emulsion layers.

lens

filter

blue
blue-green
green
yellow
orange
red

COLOR PICTURES can be made from any type of color film. Color film is available in both daylight and artificial-light types. Kodachrome II, Kodacolor, and Anscochrome Color Film are generally processed either by local commercial photo labs or by their manufacturers. Kodak Ektachrome E-2 can be processed—if care is used—in a home darkroom. Agfachrome, Kodachrome, Ektachrome, and Anscochrome Color Film are processed directly into transparencies for projection. Prints can be made from these. Kodacolor and Agfacolor make prints—transparencies can then be made but are expensive; color quality may suffer. Ektachrome E-2 is made especially for those who want to do their own developing and printing. It is fun and one can produce excellent results. (Processing kits with instructions are available.)

Reproduction from Anscochrome transparency.

Reproduction from Ektachrome transparency.

WHICH FILM TO USE is largely a matter of person-al choice. Yellows tend to disappear on some and greens are brownish on others. Experiment, find films you like, then stick with them. Build experience with one type of film and you will get better pictures. But note the great variations in speed indexes (p. 34).

Kodacolor negative   Kodacolor positive

COLOR ESSENTIALS Remember three basic points about color photography as compared to black-and-white photography:

1 Color film has less latitude (it tolerates less over- or underexposure), so making accurate exposures is important. Moderate over- and underexposure will show first as poor color rendition.

2 Color film is much slower than average black-and-white film. Kodachrome II has an index of 25, and 35 mm. Ektachrome and Anscochrome have indexes of 32—as compared with 160 for Plus X Pan. So use more generous exposures when shooting in color. (Film speeds for all color films are packed with the film.)

3 Because objects are revealed in color contrasts instead of brightness contrasts, flat front lighting is safest. As you experiment with color, you will want to try oblique lighting, too. But front lighting, with a minimum of contrast between highlights and shadows, will give you your most satisfying pictures. This is particularly important for color portraits. Harsh shadows from strong sunlight detract from the detail that improves most pictures of people.

Strong side lighting produces harsh shadows and contrast.

Front lighting avoids shadows. Color gives depth and details.

This portrait was taken with bright sunlight shining down on the girl's hat. The strong light on her face was cast by a smooth aluminum reflector held about waist height in front of the model.

The slowness of most color film requires a fast lens or long exposure in dim light. With simple cameras, concentrate on well-lighted, front-lighted subjects. Adjustable cameras provide more leeway. In general, base your exposure on the brightness of the major center of interest. If skin tones are important, adjust exposure for them. If you have an exposure meter, take a reading with your meter held close to your subject.

A good way to solve the shadow problem for color (and for black-and-white, too) is with a reflector. Get a sheet of heavy white cardboard, about 20 by 30 in. Glue crinkled aluminum foil to the back with model-plane cement to make a shiny, but un-mirrorlike surface. With such a reflector, held just out of the camera's view, you can bounce light back into the shaded side of your subject and lighten the shadows materially. The white side of the cardboard will give you a soft diffused light; the foil side will give a stronger, brighter illumination. Reflectors are useful, too, with artificial lighting (pp. 86-87). Flash also can soften shadows (pp. 82-83).

DAY AND NIGHT IN COLOR The time of day makes a big difference in the color of sunlight and in the color photos you take. Sunrise or sunset light is ruddy. At early or late hours a white house, a sandy beach, or a person will photograph reddish. The light midday hours give truer colors provided colorful nearby buildings, fences, trees, etc. do not reflect light on your subject. Such light can do strange things. Pose a girl under rich foliage and her skin tones will reflect the green of the leaves.

No two of us see color exactly alike, and very few have accurate colory memory. Remember this in judging color prints or transparencies. Over- or underexposure may throw colors askew, but the color in your pictures may be more accurate than your memory of the scene.

Use the right film for the light if you want color accuracy. Daylight film is balanced for the relatively blue-white sunlight. If you use it at night under the yellow-red light of photofloods or ordinary flashbulbs, you'll get reddish results. If you use indoor-type film for sunlit shots, you get excess blues.

Midday shots—colors normal

Early or late shots—reddish

Wet pavement reflects the bright lights of Times Square on a rainy night. The photographer used Ektachrome Film, and exposed 1 sec. at f/4, using a bus stop sign for a tripod.

Norman-Prange Pictures

Under emergency conditions you can use daylight color film with flash by using a blue-coated flash bulb. But don't try daylight film with floods unless you use a photoflood filter (Wratten No. 80B). Even this will produce some color shift, so stick to the correct film if possible.

It's less of a problem to use indoor-type films (such as Kodachrome II or Anscochrome) for daylight shooting. With a Wratten No. 85 filter, your results will be much the same as with daylight films. Of course, the proper film is always better.

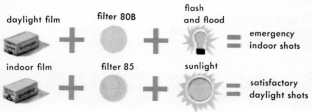

daylight film + filter 80B + flash and flood = emergency indoor shots

indoor film + filter 85 + sunlight = satisfactory daylight shots

POLAROID COLOR FILM gives you color prints in less than a minute (time varies with temperature). Usable in most Polaroid cameras (p. 98), Polacolor film is a technical miracle and a photographer's delight. Color rendition is excellent. Conventional color film requires over 20 steps to process the negative and make a print. This takes over 90 minutes of darkroom work plus the time required to send your film to a laboratory and get it back. Polacolor film is radically different. Take your picture, pull a tab, wait 50 seconds, and lift out your finished picture. A complex one-step chemical process goes on automatically in your film while you wait. You see your finished picture at once.

Polacolor film contains everything needed to make a color print—negative, positive, developer, fixer, hardener, and wash. A complex system of linked dyes and developer molecules migrate from negative to positive to produce the final print. Chemicals in the positive part of the film even "wash" out the print and seal the dyes in a tough, clear layer.

COMPARISON OF POLACOLOR AND CONVENTIONAL COLOR PRINTS

POLACOLOR	CONVENTIONAL
One processing step goes on automatically when tab is pulled.	More than 20 processing steps in developing negative and making color print. All done in darkroom.
Processing time about 50 seconds (varies with temperature).	51 minutes required to get negative plus 42 minutes for print.
All dyes are built into negative when film is made. These migrate to positive automatically.	No dyes are built into film. Two sets of dyes are made during processing—one in negative and one in positive.
Print is made by migration of linked dye molecules from negative to positive in film.	Print made by exposing printing paper to light through developed negative.

Polaroid Land Color Print

Polacolor Print, 2½" by 3¼" (actual size)

POLACOLOR FILM TECHNICAL DATA

Film Speed Index 75 when temperatures are above 60 degrees. Speed drops at lower temperatures, rises at higher; e.g., at 45 degrees, speed is 25.

Development time 50 sec. for most pictures, longer time at lower temperatures, less at higher. Example: 90 secs. at 45 degrees.

Flash pictures Use blue flashbulbs or electronic flash.

Sizes available Type 48 film for 3¼ X 4¼ pictures for all 40-series Polaroid Land cameras. Type 38 film for 2½ X 3¼ pictures for all J33 models. Models 80, 80A, and 80B Polaroid Land cameras require factory conversion.

Comparative cost All Polacolor film is packed 6 exposures to a roll. Polacolor film is a little over twice the cost of Polaroid black-and-white film.

Copies and enlargements 3¼ X 4¼ copy prints available from Polaroid Corporation. (2½ X 3¼ prints are copied in 3¼ X 4¼ size) 5" X 7" and 8" X 10" enlargements also made by Polaroid.

51

Phoebe Dunn

▲ Avoid strong color contrasts, unless you want carnival-looking shots. This picture shows good color balance.

Learn to look for reflected overtones—the blues, violets, greens, and yellows that often lie like a thin wash over landscapes. Your sensitive film will pick up these colors. Train your eye to see them, too, in order to get the best range of tones in color shots. ▼

TIPS ON COLOR Exposure is all-important. Follow directions on film. An exposure meter is a help in color work.

▲ Compose your shots so that color works for you. Use strong colors sparingly as accents to emphasize your point of interest.

▲ Use a soft front lighting and avoid shadows. Your eye sees details that the film can't get. Shadows and dark lines will be darker on your film than they appear to your eye. Use reflectors or avoid shadows.

Ken Weith—Popular Photography

All Kinds of Pictures

Every picture situation presents a different problem. Candid photography is very different from portrait work. Picturing babies requires tricks unneeded in taking pictures of adults—who present their own problems! The following pages offer advice to help you on the main kinds of problems and provide examples of what can be done to solve them. All the types of pictures in this section can be taken with a box camera. More elaborate cameras increase the chances of better results but are not essential. By careful experimenting, you can gradually bring to your picture-taking something worth far more than a better lens or an extra gadget. You can bring experience, understanding, and intelligent composition—without which the best camera is inferior. The following pages present suggestions you should follow closely at first. As you gain experience, experiment.

COMPOSING YOUR PICTURE 1 Avoid cutting your picture in two by putting the horizon across the middle. A third of the way up or down is about right.

2 A picture in which the subject appears squarely in the middle tends to come to life if the subject is placed a third of the way in from top or bottom, and a third of the way in from either side. Divide your scene into thirds, up and down and across. The points where the lines cross are good places to set your subject.

3 Think of the sides of your picture as walls and you'll naturally avoid having people facing, walking into, or even looking directly at one of the walls.

Paul Richards—Scholastic-Ansco Photography Awards

Shapes and lines are important in planning the composition of your pictures.

4 Sharp angles like those of T, Y, L, V, N, and Z tend to create moods of rigidity, strength, and harshness. Use them accordingly.

5 Generally speaking, S and C curves provide a flowing, graceful feeling. Use them to create moods of quiet, gentleness, and flowing motion.

6 Horizontal lines such as walls or roads are seldom interesting if they appear horizontally in your pictures. Take them at an angle so that they go diagonally.

7 Remember that shadows and background are a part of the composition. Make shadows work for you. Dramatic pictures can be made of light patterns as such.

O. E. Nelson—Popular Photography
Bleakness of city snow storm

Pilings provide depth.

SCENES AND VISTAS should create a mood. The mood itself is the heart of your subject, whatever the view. What is it that makes you want the picture? Is it the mists rising off the lake? The rich peace of an autumn landscape? Analyze your feelings and work to get a picture that catches that mood.

Most scenes present no depth-of-field problem because you are focused on a distant view. There is little or no motion, so you can use a slow shutter speed and a stopped-down lens if your camera permits. For medium or contrasting sky tone, use a yellow or red filter.

Study the scene, then move around until you get the best angle, the best placement of your major point of interest, the most effective pattern of light and shadow. Foreground detail will help give your picture depth.

For mood, try a snowstorm. Some of the most dramatic shots are taken during rain, sleet, snow, and windstorms.

Reflections add to tranquil mood.

Lighthouse against afternoon sk

▲ To capture the beauty of any scene on film, the photographer must be able to translate his feelings into the technical medium of the camera. Lighting, lens opening, shutter speed, focus—control of these factors results in the desired effect caught on Kodachrome at 1/25 and f/11 for good depth.

This snowscape was taken on Kodachrome at 1 sec. and f/16. ▼

TIPS FOR SCENIC PICTURES Foreground material gives depth. Don't stand at the edge of a cliff to catch that awesome drop. Step back and frame the view with a bush. Which of the two pictures at the top gives you the greater feeling of depth and distance? It takes something in the foreground to give that "3-D" effect.

Don't forget filters: clouds almost always improve a scenic picture. The first picture below was taken with a K2 filter, and the clouds appear natural. The second was taken with an A filter; the clouds are brooding. Use the red filter if you want to obtain stormy effects, and the yellow if you want sunny effects.

Shadows are important for depth. Your best scenes will rarely be taken at noon, when shadows are shortest. Side-light or back-light your scenes wherever possible. Long shadows to the side or toward you create depth and texture. Compare pictures above. Use a lens hood or hold a piece of cardboard over your lens to avoid light streaks when shooting into the sun.

Keep it simple! Don't let your landscapes be cluttered up with things that distract attention from the subject. Move around, get nearer—anything to avoid those obstacles that stick up in bad pictures. You can't arrange a landscape or building, but you can get the best angle.

Hedrich-Blessing Studio

Camera angle enhanced the beauty of this house.

THIS IS WHERE I LIVE You've heard the statement "Pictures don't lie." It isn't true. Pictures, by their very nature, report only a selected part of what your eyes see. So if your camera tells only part of the truth, why not make it tell the part that you want it to?

When you picture your home, it can be excusably glamorized. Search for the best angle. Wait until the sun casts flattering shadows. Shoot to include shrubbery. A foreground shrub or tree can give the idea that your home nestles in a veritable park. Screen out your neigh-

Stark—bad camera angle

Same house—beauty emphasize

Hedrich-Blessing Studio

Shadows emphasize architectural detail.

bors by shooting from an angle so that shrubbery masks their homes. You want to show your house, not the neighborhood. Wash on the line and garbage cans are home necessities, but leave them out of your picture—unless you have good reason for including them. If your house faces north, it gets little sunlight. Settle for a semi-overcast day when the shadows are soft.

It's your house, your home. If you'll take a little time to compose your shot, look for the best angle, and wait for the right time of day, others will love it too.

Keep your foreground clear.   Foreground adds value here.

Paul Weller

Balanced light is the key to good interior exposures.

INTERIOR EXPOSURES Most all interiors are, to your camera, fairly dark scenes broken up by overly brilliant areas—sunny windows, doors, and patches of sunlight. Interiors are generally too dark for snapshots, and the uneven lighting makes time exposures difficult.

The job with interior pictures is to level off the lighting as much as you can. Aim away from the sunny spots that will give a room a broken-up effect; make use of the diffuse light from non-sunny windows in the room.

For a good interior time exposure, a tripod or other firm camera support is necessary. Cut the lens opening down

North-lighted windows are safe.

Sunny spots can add interest.

to its minimum setting to give fullest depth of field. Usually, a time exposure of 1 to 5 sec. will do the job with black-and-white film unless the room is very dark. Good pictures in average-size rooms can be taken near a window at 1/50 at about f/5.6 with Kodak Tri-X Film. Experiment with a range of exposures.

Set your camera at eye level to give a normal view of the interior. Arrange furniture invitingly with a foreground piece placed so that your camera can view over it, to give scale and perspective. Too much furniture will make your picture cluttered—so move some out of range.

Watch out for bright reflections in glass cupboards, on the shiny side of a piano, or in the glass of framed pictures —another reason for choosing a hazy day. If you can't avoid reflections, use a Polaroid polarizing filter. Don't try to get the entire room in one picture. Your regular lens can't see very far to the sides. Try several angles. With more expensive cameras, use a wide-angle lens (p. 100).

Normal lighting caught this railroad station at f/4.5 and 1/25.

Doris Pinney—Popular Photography

Lights of moving cars leave streaks.

NIGHT EXPOSURES are rewarding. Time exposures with rock-steady camera open for 2 min. or more are needed with most films. But high speed film such as Tri-X will take bright home interiors or brightly lit city street scenes at 1/25 sec. with about f/3.5 (Take several shots at different exposures to insure getting a good picture). High Speed Ektachrome or Super Anscochrome can get stage shows at about 1/60 sec. at f/2.8. Try these films at 3 sec. at f/8 for *brightly* lit night shots. Exposed lights record easily with time exposures. A moving car leaves a streak of white light coming and red light going.

◄ Night lends beauty and mystery to ordinary street scenes. Try shooting them with both black-and-white and color film. This scene was shot on Verichrome Pan Film, 30 sec. at f/8. Ordinary street lights provided the only illumination. Same shot in Kodacolor would require 1½ min. at f/8.

Sunset captured on Kodachrome. exposure ½ sec. at f/16.

In town wet nights are fine for photography. City streets will appear deserted—except for those pedestrians who pause near by to light a cigarette. If you want people to show, have them stand still during your exposure.

In the country, with few artificial lights, exposures have to be much longer. Even under bright moonlight, exposures of 10 min. or more are normal. For most night shots, leave your lens wide open; depth of field will seldom be a problem. For sunsets with Kodachrome II or comparable color film, try ¼ sec. to 1 sec. at f/16. With High Speed Ektachrome B you can hand-hold camera.

Oil refinery becomes fairyland in nighttime exposure.

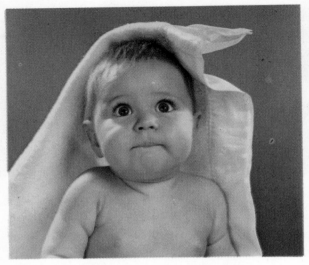
Soft lighting adds naturalness to baby pictures.

BABIES Baby pictures should be—and can be—charming. First, don't try to direct. Any baby knows more about charm than we do. Second, use soft lighting. Open shade outdoors is ideal, as on the shaded side of a house on a bright day. It may require a little more exposure, but don't slow down below 1/50 sec. Babies are unpredictable and quick. Third, watch your background. Keep it simple. A wall is better than a cluttered garage. Fourth, keep your distance. If you must get closer than 5 or 6 ft. for a box camera and about 3 ft. for most focusing cameras, use an accessory lens (portrait lens that slips over your present lens).

Be patient! With camera ready, wait for the baby to do something appealing. Give him a toy and let his interest center on it. Let him forget you, while you concentrate on a series of shots at various angles and levels.

CHILDREN Moving up the age scale from babies to children, basic picture techniques change very little. Establish a generous area for your operations (kids don't stay put) and give your subjects something to watch or play with—a pet, a gadget, a favorite doll. Once you've established the basic situation, concentrate quietly on your camera. Better yet, wait until children are absorbed in their own play. Then, make yourself at home until they've forgotten you and your camera. Keep a group of children busy with some common interest. Otherwise, they'll stand stiffly in an ungainly, grinning line.

Use a fairly fast shutter speed and rely more on watchful patience than on technique to get those outstanding shots. **TIP:** If you want your subjects to look at you, say "Hi!" or call their names and then snap. You'll get alert expressions every time. You can't use it too often with the same children, of course.

Give him something to do—then shoot.

Absorption of this pair emphasized by busy station.

ADULTS Many people are shy and freeze before a camera. So face the problem as in picturing children. De-emphasize the camera and get your subject to concentrate on some activity or interest. Something to hold in the hands is useful—a book, a flower, anything that's in character.

As to lighting, strong sunshine creates contrasts. Relieve the shadows by light reflected from a sunny wall, white sand, or a prepared white reflector (p. 47). Use direct sunlight with strong shadows for character studies of strong, rugged, interesting faces; otherwise, use the hazy, overcast light—it's much more flattering.

Watch your setting; keep the background simple and uncluttered. Sky is hard to beat for a simple, effective background. And don't forget the value of filters (pp. 35-37). They can be used to improve skin texture and for dramatic shots against the sky.

Never say "Smile, please"—for the resulting expressions are never what you want in a picture! Sometimes chatting with your subject will help him relax.

Keep background simple and subjects busy for better portraits.

◀ The low camera angle helped the effect in this picture.

Hal Berg

Phoebe Dunn

The bright colors add to the candid effect of this scene. ▶

The trick in candid photos is to catch your subject unaware.

STREET SCENES AND CANDID SHOTS   Most people are at their natural best when unaware of observation. So a small, fast-lensed, inconspicuous camera is a help. But you can get good unposed shots with any camera, even a simple fixed-focus, fixed-speed type.

Try some street scenes. A traffic cop, pedestrians waiting for the light to change, window shoppers, newsboys—the possibilities are endless. Don't fuss with meters. Operate at a reasonable distance—say, 10 ft.—and set your camera at hyperfocal distance (p. 27) with your lens stopped down as much as the available light will allow at a speed of 1/50 sec. Once you get your camera set, don't alter it unless lighting conditions change drastically. Don't worry about composition. You are after character studies—interesting faces and interesting stories.

If your camera makes your game wary, wander around a bit without using the camera until suspicion fades. That's your chance: use it. You may even have to resort to the old trick of pretending interest in something well to one side of your subject while you shoot with camera directed at him. Train yourself to look in unusual places for your story. The feet of people watching a parade might tell a better story than their faces.

Keep your sense of decency and good taste. People resent being pictured if they are in any way handicapped, either physically or economically. Never sell a candid, unposed picture for publication unless your subject has agreed to such use in writing. Publication of such pictures without a written release or permission constitutes an invasion of privacy, and you can easily land in court, subject to suit for damages.

Set camera at hyperfocal distance for street scenes.

Paul Weller

Silhouette with setting sun as back-light. Kodachrome, 1/50 at f/8.

SILHOUETTES FOR DRAMA

Use light from behind your subject to get an outline with little detail—a silhouette.

If the light source is low, as at sunset, you'll get very little shadow detail. With midafternoon sunlight you'll have much well-lighted detail beyond your foreground silhouette. Both can be highly dramatic; the latter can create a fine sense of depth to a picture. Normally you need no drastic change in exposure; but underexpose just a bit so that your exposure is correct mainly for the highlights.

Many "moonlight" scenes across water are taken in the early mornings or late afternoons. Shoot toward the sun and deliberately underexpose—the reflection of sunlight on the water will give a moonlit look. Try the same for wet streets on a sunny late afternoon. In all silhouette shots, shade your lens from direct rays of light with a lens hood or cardboard to avoid light flares.

Frame public buildings with back-lighted foregrounds to achieve dramatic effects. Choose your camera angle carefully and compose for good balance. This scene was shot on Verichrome Pan, 1/50 sec. at f/16.

The Hansel and Gretel quality of this picture results almost entirely from silhouette effect of tiny figures bathed in pool of sunlight streaming into dense woodland. Verichrome Pan was exposed at 1/50, f/11 for sunny highlights, so dark background is black.

This "moonlight" shot was taken in daylight. Camera was pointed toward sunlight reflected from water. Underexposed, on Verichrome Pan at 1/100 and f/16, dark canoe is silhouetted against bright patch of water as if it were in bright moonlight.

DON'T MAKE THESE MISTAKES To learn from your mistakes you must be able to recognize what has gone wrong. The next four pages illustrate the most common blunders of photography. Get out your prints. Find any that look like the pictures on these pages? The captions will help you find out what went wrong and how to avoid repeating that mistake.

◄ **Bad focus** Can't happen with box or other cameras with pre-set focus unless you get too near. Keep 6 ft. away or use a close-up lens. With adjustable-focus cameras without rangefinders, measure distances when subject is close.

Dirty lens Looks something like a poorly focused shot. You can tell the difference, though, because part of the subject is distinct and clear. Clean lens with camera-lens tissue and lens cleaner. ►

◄ **Camera moved** Everything is blurred. A poor focus shot usually has a distinct background. Use tripod for exposures less than 1/25 sec. and squeeze the shutter release.

Subject moved The subject is blurred, but the background is distinct. You usually know it isn't bad focus on subject because part of the body moved more slowly, so is fairly distinct. ▶

◄ Camera tilted Compose your subject through your viewer and you'll avoid shots like this. Keep looking until you've snapped your picture.

Subject scalped A common result of not watching subject through viewer until after you've shot. Compose carefully, hold camera steady, trip shutter smoothly, and you'll avoid shots like this one. ▶

◄ Double exposure Did you advance the film after that last shot? If you didn't, you'll get double exposures. Shoot and advance film immediately.

All photographs, except double exposure, are by Joseph Foldes, reproduced courtesy Popular Photography.

75

Overexposed pictures are thin and have a washed-out look. Cut down diaphragm or increase shutter speed. Keep a record of your exposures and learn from them. ▶

◀ **Underexposed pictures** are dark and often muddy looking. Open up diaphragm or cut down shutter speed. If your pictures are like this or that above, try an exposure meter.

Light flare most commonly results from a leak in the camera case. Don't try to fix it yourself. Occasional light flares are probably from reflected glare or sun shining on the lens. Polaroid polarizing filter for first, lens shade for second. ▶

◀ **Flat lighting** Mistake of beginners. The subjects, facing into the sun, have to squint. Glare paints out all detail, leaving a flat picture. Remember: sun over shoulder or open shade.

Distracting background is a fault to be avoided by posing the subject in a better setting, or by opening up the diaphragm in order to reduce your depth of field. ▶

◀ **No story** is the worst blunder of all. What's the photographer trying to tell us? Whatever it was, he's lost it. Compose so your subject stands out. Avoid distractions.

No blunders here—a picture worth having. ▼

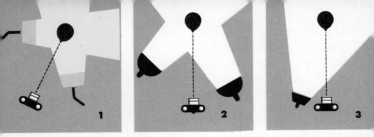

1 **Normal home lighting** For portraits, place two 100-watt bulbs 2 to 3 ft. from subject. Try ½ sec. at f/11 on fast pan film.

2 **Photoflood** arrangement is a basic plan. Left light is 5 ft. from subject. Right light is 7 ft. from subject and closer to camera.

3 **Flash** lighting is harsh when flash is attached to camera as shown. Pages 82-83 show other arrangements.

Lighting Your Pictures

Photographs are light pictures. Light conditions determine your shutter speed and lens setting. Now see what you can do to control the light itself. Our suggestions so far have generally assumed natural lighting—sunlight, direct and indirect. For many purposes, natural lighting can't be bettered. But you don't have to put your camera away at night; it can work then as well as by day.

Artificial light gives you the chance at real light control. You can shoot any time, day or night—and you can get shots which are impossible with natural lighting. Time exposures with regular light bulbs will do for interiors at night. But when you want to catch people in action—a party, Mother sewing, or Dad getting his fishing tackle ready for vacation next month—flash is the answer. And for portraits in which the tones are perfect and every shadow is just right, you will want to use photofloods. Ordinary house lights, flash, and photofloods—now let's see how these types of lighting are used and controlled.

PICTURES WITH HOME LIGHTS

The main problem you face in taking interiors at night is correct exposure. Interior lighting is so dim that exposure meters are of little help.

In a medium-size room, with light walls and ceiling and the equivalent of three 100-watt lamps, try Tri-X and expose at 1/25 at f/3.5. With ordinary fast pan, try 10 sec. at f/11 to f/16. Experiment with different exposures (8, 10, 12, 15 sec.).

A seated person can hold still for 10 to 15 sec. For close-ups, place two 100-watt bulbs within 2 or 3 ft. of your subject. With fast film, ½ sec. at f/11 should do the job. Here are three pictures taken with ordinary lighting. Note the exposures.

Available light provides a natural quality and softness not obtainable with flash. Try it with Kodak Tri-X and other fast films.

Kodachrome and one 300-w. bulb

Allan Green—Popular Photography
Tri-X Film and one 60-w. bulb

Two 300-w. bulbs, 1/25 at f/3.5

NOW ADD FLASH! Flash lamps can be used only once. But they are indispensable in certain situations where there is action and poor illumination. Flash lamps come in various sizes. The simplest (No. 22) screws into an ordinary lamp socket. Place the lamp a little higher than your subject and point it slightly downward; set your camera for time or bulb; turn out the room lights; open the shutter; set off the flash bulb by the lamp switch; close the shutter. You can use this open-flash method with any kind of camera.

Most modern cameras—even box cameras—have a built-in flash synchronizer. All you have to do is click the shutter to set off the flash. But not all flash-synchronized shutters will work with all types of flash bulbs. Check the directions for your camera before buying flash bulbs.

Important: Flash bulbs are coated with a lacquer to keep them from shattering; but they can break. Cover the bulb with a plastic protector or handkerchief when making close-ups, and increase your exposure considerably.

WHAT EXPOSURE WITH FLASH? There are guide numbers for each type and kind of flash bulb for each type of film and shutter speed. To find the right lens setting, select the correct guide number and divide it by the distance in feet from the flash bulb to the subject. For example, the guide number for a No. 5 lamp with Kodak Plus-X Film and a shutter speed of 1/50 is 170. If the distance to the subject is 10 ft., divide 170 by 10; so f/17 or f/16 is indicated. Guides come with film and bulbs.

Sun-Lite II

Kodak Motormatic 35F
with pop-up flash

Sun-Lite "500"

Hal Berg—Popular Photography

Simulated natural light with electronic flash

FLASH-EXPOSURE GUIDE NUMBERS
FOR NO. 5 OR 25 BULBS (With 4 to 5 inch reflectors)
Black-and-White Film (Clear bulbs)

FILM	SHUTTER SPEED			
	1/25 to 1/30	1/50 to 1/60	1/100 to 1/125	1/200 to 1/250
Kodak				
Panatomic-X	200	180	160	120
Verichrome Pan	280	260	220	180
Plus-X	300	280	240	180
Tri-X	550	500	440	360
Ansco				
Super Hypan	540	460	380	260
All-Weather Pan	200	180	160	120
Color Films				
Kodak				
Kodachrome II (blue bulbs)	80	70	65	50
Kodachrome-X (blue bulbs)	140	110	100	75
Ektachrome (blue bulbs)	110	100	90	70
Ektachrome-X (blue bulbs)	140	110	100	75
Kodacolor (clear bulbs)	120	110	95	70
Kodacolor-X (clear bulbs)	180	150	130	100
Ansco				
Anscochrome (blue bulbs)	100	95	75	55
Super Ansco. (blue bulbs)	175	170	130	95

Flash on camera gives harsh shadows and loss of detail.

PLACING THE FLASH BULB Most users of flash are content to operate with the flash attached directly to the camera, so their pictures are strictly front-lighted, with a thin edge of shadow outlining the off side of the subject. This may throw a harsh light on your subject—much like that of direct sunlight. With some flash outfits, extension flashes can be attached to give more than one source of light. This will tone down strong shadows and give extra softening light. Another way to soften flash is to place a white handkerchief, or other diffuser, over reflector.

Flash on extension   Handkerchief over flash

Using bounce lighting with your flash will give more even lighting to portraits and cast flattering shadows.

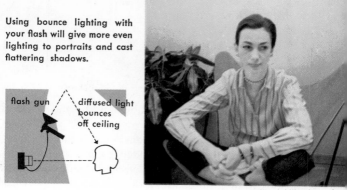

Herschel Wartik

Some flash outfits can be detached from the camera and held a foot or more away. With such equipment you can bounce light off the ceiling, a nearby light-colored wall, or a reflector. This will avoid harshness and is ideal for portraits. Note the picture above made with bounce light. Because the light travels farther, you have to provide a more generous exposure. Exactly how much more depends on the distance to the bounce surface and its brightness. Placed low and shining up, flash can give a firelight effect; placed inside a window or door frame, it simulates sunlight streaming in.

Flash put in fireplace.

Flash simulates candlelight.

Electronic Flash

Graflite Jr. B-C Flash

MORE ON FLASH The bugaboo of flash is the failure of the little dry-cells at just the wrong time. Fresh batteries for every picture-making expedition are advisable. Freedom from uncertainty is provided by B-C (battery-condenser) flash outfits. Tiny hearing-aid batteries are used, but the current is stored for instant use in a small electrical condenser. It's swift and certain—long-lived, too.

Electronic flashes (strobe lights) are a totally different type of flash unit. Amateurs are using them in increasing numbers, for they have several advantages over conventional flash. For one thing, the electronic lamp is good for 10,000 or so shots instead of one. The units are fairly expensive, but the lamp life cuts the cost over a period of years. Second, the flashes are much faster—that's where the real advantage lies. Ordinary flash lamps fire in from 1/75 to 1/200 sec.—fast enough for ordinary work. But electronic flash fires in about 1/500 to 1/5000 sec.—fast enough to stop almost anything. Look at the sample shots below. Both were taken with electronic flash units.

Strobe of splashing milk drop
Harold E. Edgerton

Impact of ball and racquet
Harold E. Edgerton

PHOTOFLOODS should be used if you want professional lighting effects—especially for portraits (pp. 86-89). Of several types of photofloods, the most commonly used are No. 1, No. 2, RFL 2 (with built-in reflector), and RSP 2 (with built-in spot reflector).

Caution: More than three 500-watt photofloods on a single house circuit will blow the fuses.

All photofloods screw into ordinary light sockets. Reflectors (p. 47), required with No. 1 and No. 2, throw intense light where you want it. Photofloods are less brilliant than flash, so longer exposures are required. Use tripod for speeds less than 1/50 sec. Check settings with light meter or use table below.

FLOOD EXPOSURES WITH TWO R2 PHOTOFLOODS

FILM	DISTANCE IN FT. — LAMPS TO SUBJECT					
	3½*&5	4*&6	5*&7	7*&9	8*&12	15*&15*
Kodak						
Verichrome Pan	--	1/25	--	1/25	1/25	1/25
	--	f/11	--	f/8	f/6.3	f/4
Tri-X	1/25	--	1/25	1/25	--	1/25
	f/22	--	f/16	f/11	--	f/6.3
Panatomic X	1/25	--	1/25	1/25	--	--
	f/8	--	f/5.6	f/4	--	--
Ektachrome Film Type F**	1/25	1/25	1/25	--	--	--
	f/4.5	f/4	f/3.2	--	--	--
Kodachrome Film Type F**	1/2	1/2	1/2	1/2	1/2	1/2
	f/11–	f/11	f/8–	f/6.3	f/5.6	f/2.8
	f/16	--	f/11	--	--	--
Kodacolor Film**	1/25	1/25	1/25	1/25	--	--
	f/5.6	f/4.5	f/4	f/2.8	--	--
**With Kodak Light Balancing Filter No. 82A						
Ansco						
All-Weather Pan	1/25	1/25	1/25	1/25	1/25	1/25
	f/12.5	f/11	f/8	f/6.3	f/5.6	f/3.5
Super Hypan	1/25	1/25	1/25	1/25	1/25	1/25
	f/17	f/15	f/12	f/8.5	f/7.5	f/4
Anscochrome (3200K) Tungsten	1/25	1/25	1/25	1/25	1/10	1/5
	f/5	f/4.5	f/4	f/3.5	f/4	f/3.5

For color films, place both lamps at distance marked*.

Randolph-Delong

PHOTOFLOOD PORTRAITS

Good portraits are a joy and a challenge. Experiment with the lighting ideas that follow. Because photofloods are hot and bright, use a big doll or statuette for experimenting. Keep settings simple. A drapery about 3 ft. back of "Anna"—a milliner's mannequin—forms the background of the experimental pictures on the opposite page. Study these pictures first.

For a basic photoflood lighting plan, consult the table on p. 85. Use fast pan film to start with. Adding back lighting won't change the exposure—it gives accents only. With a meter you can figure exposure for any combination of lights if the table is not sufficient.

First try placing your camera about 8 ft. from your subject. Your main light—No. 2 in reflector or RFL 2—is put about 5 ft. from the subject and at an angle of about 45° to a line from subject to camera. Place just about face level. Now comes the fill-in light—another No. 2 or RFL 2 —to lighten the shadows cast by the main light. Place about 7 ft. from subject, close to camera, and on the side away from the main light. This is the basic lighting plan for all portraits, but it is flexible. Try raising the main light 1 or 2 ft. Note how it produces eye shadow, more shape to the chin, a little better modeling. Experiment with the angles and distances. Notice how mood changes with high and low light angles.

Next try lights as shown on the next page. Besides the main and fill-in lights, add others, or a white sheet or cardboard reflectors. A commonly used third light is a spot aimed down from behind the subject to give luster to the hair—a slight halo effect that is often attractive.

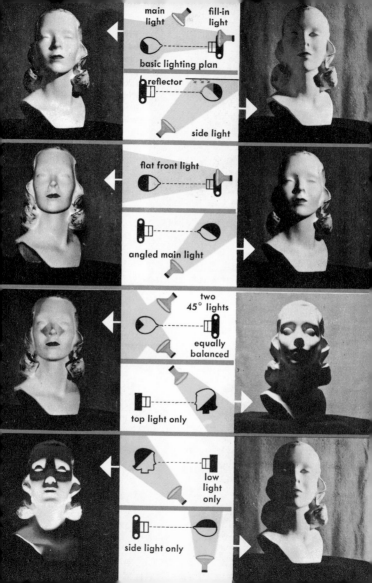

main light   fill-in light

basic lighting plan

reflector

side light

flat front light

angled main light

two 45° lights

equally balanced

top light only

low light only

side light only

FINE PORTRAITS can be taken with any kind of camera or lighting. The portrait to the left was taken with Ektachrome Film. One lamp was behind and above the camera. See diagram below for lighting plan.

Philippe Halsman—Magnum

Candid effect with strobe flash

Paul Weller

Two flashes give rounded feeling.

Rus Arnold—Popular Photography

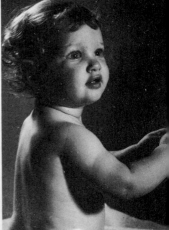

Softer and more even lighting was used to obtain the old-fashioned quality of this picture. Four floods with reflectors, one directed at background, were used. Light arrangement is shown below. Exposure: f/5.6 at 1/30 sec.

Phoebe Dunn

Available light will give you sharper contrasts in portraits.

Paul Weller

89

All About Cameras

Cameras are basically alike. Any kind will take good pictures if you know how to use it. Simple auxiliary equipment—such as filters, close-up lenses, and flash—turn even inexpensive box cameras into versatile instruments which will take good pictures under almost any conditions.

There is no ideal camera. Cameras made for all-purpose use are poor for some specialized uses. On the other hand, a camera designed to take portraits would be hard to use for action shots. Weigh the advantages and disadvantages of each type of camera. You will be happiest with a camera that meets your own particular needs.

Cameras are of eight different types or combinations of types. Each has advantages and disadvantages. Following are some basic facts about each type.

Box camera

Press camera

Twin-lens reflex camera

Stereo Realist

Polaro
Automatic 100 Land Came

Single-lens reflex camera

Folding camera

Miniature camera

Ansco Cadet II
with flash

Argus 75
with flash

Brownie Reflex 20

Brownie Super 27
with built-in flash

Kodak Instamatic 100
with flash

BOX CAMERAS, with simple lens and fixed aperture and shutter speed, are the easiest cameras to use. All use roll film—black-and-white or color. As a group, they are the least expensive cameras. Simplicity makes them almost foolproof—especially Kodak Instamatic with a pre-loaded film cartridge that clicks into camera back. Most have flash attachments and take filters and closeup lenses. Reflex type has a second lens for viewing through a screen. Box cameras take average pictures under average conditions.

Advantages Inexpensive: mass production and big sales make box cameras the best buy for the money. These are good cameras and will take good pictures.

Foolproof: Simple construction, minimum controls. Anyone can take good pictures under average conditions.

Rugged: Will take considerable abuse. Best cameras for children.

Disadvantages Lack of versatility: fixed lens setting, aperture, and shutter speed prohibit picture taking under extreme conditions of light, motion, depth.

Simple lens: impossible to get sharp detail under many conditions.

91

Leica M3 with
Leica-meter "MC"

Nikon SP

Vitomatic IIA

Contax with
telephoto lens

THE MIGHTY MINIATURES

Light and compact, these are the best cameras for fast shooting under a wide range of conditions. Most take inexpensive 35 mm. roll film — black-and-white or color—and make standard 2 by 2 in. color slides for projection. (Kodak Instamatic Cameras use film in cartridges for foolproof loading even in bright light.)

Extremely fast lenses—you can get them at f/2 or even faster—make it possible to get pictures unobtainable with slower lenses. A wide variety of attachments is available for many miniatures. With close-up rings or bellows you can shoot a small object life size. Microscope attachments open an invisible world to the camera. The telephoto lens brings distant scenes into range. Special equipment makes underwater photography possible. For versatility and compactness, get a miniature.

Argus Standard C3

Kodak Instamatic 700
with flash

Advantages Light and compact, easy to carry. Inconspicuous and quick to adjust—best cameras for candid work. Short focal-length lens (usually 50 mm.) gives extreme depth of field and makes precise focusing unnecessary for that once-in-a-lifetime shot that won't wait. Fastest lenses of any type still camera; invaluable for action shots in dim light, for street scenes, and for shooting at theater. Lowest film cost and largest number of shots per loading (20 or 36 shots per cartridge). Highly versatile. Wide range of attachments and accessories for some brands.

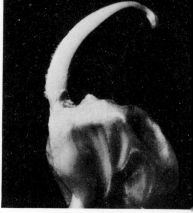

Germinating corn, f/22, 15 sec.

Display case taken by miniature.

Cornell-Capa—Magnum

Disadvantages Large film load makes most 35 mms. impractical for single shoot-and-develop technique. Enlargements necessary for prints—meaning inevitable loss of detail and sharpness. Care required in big enlargements: smallest film scratch becomes noticeable on print. Parallax problem on close-ups (see p. 96) except with single-lens reflex miniatures or those with parallax correction.

Tiger lily, f/11 and 1/25.

Bright fungus, f/8 and 1/100.

PRESS AND VIEW CAMERAS Press cameras are the most versatile of all. That is why they are the cameras most commonly used by news photographers (miniatures and reflexes come next in popularity). Did you ever take a picture of a tall building and have it come out looking like a pyramid? Press and view cameras can correct for such distortion by means of a swinging lens and swinging back which keep the film parallel to the subject. Negatives are large and, with good lens, provide pin-point detail which is not lost by the necessity of enlarging. But the cameras are bulky and heavy, and the film is comparatively expensive because it is large.

Advantages Fast frame or ground-glass focusing for precision. Bellows permits extreme close-ups without attachments. No, or little, enlargement of negatives necessary; superb portraits and detail possible. Change to any lens you want. These rugged cameras are extremely versatile—the do-anything cameras.

Disadvantages Bulky, heavy, and conspicuous. Inconvenient to carry around and impossible to hide if you're interested in catching your subject unaware and relaxed. Despite their use by pressmen, they're slow to operate. Film is expensive, film holders bulky. Film packs handier but cost even more. (Some take cheaper roll film.)

Herald Tribune photo, by Nat Fein. Pulitzer Prize in Photography, 1949.

Speed Graphic

Linhof
Super Technika 23

Busch 45

FOLDING CAMERAS   **FOLDING CAMERAS** These popular cameras are compact, rugged, and simple to operate. The inexpensive models are a step above the box cameras, having the advantage of adjustable controls and greater compactness. They usually take roll film, 120 and 620 being the most popular varieties. The negatives are big enough for contact prints and are fine for enlargements. The best folding cameras have fine lenses, multi-speed shutters, and all the adjustments you're likely to need. Their cost is proportionately high.

Super Ikonta IV

Speedex

Advantages Compact, light, simple to operate and generally inexpensive. Make excellent snap cameras. More expensive models capable of taking pictures with razor-sharp detail. Larger film makes satisfactory enlargements; easier than 35 mm.

Bessa II

Disadvantages There is a parallax problem on close-ups (see p. 96); they do not have interchangeable lenses; the folding mechanism can lose its rigidity.

95

Single-lens reflex uses same lens for viewing and taking pictures.

REFLEX CAMERAS Some are miniatures (35 mm.) and some are large—but they all have one thing in common and it constitutes their chief advantage. You see exactly what you are taking. This permits perfect composition and focusing.

Single-lens reflex cameras A mirror throws the image up on a ground-glass viewer the same size as the negative. When you click the shutter, the mirror flips up and the light hits the film. One big advantage over twin-lens reflex and conventional 35 mm. is that you have no parallax (difference between what you view and what you get because the viewing lens or finder is in a different position from film lens). Important for extreme close-ups.

Advantages The 35 mm. type has all the advantages of conventional miniatures—plus reflex viewing. Light, compact, fast shooting, extreme depth of field, excellent fast lenses, high versatility.

Disadvantages Same as for other 35 mm. cameras (except for larger models). Difficult to focus in dim light and with lens opening cut down (except for models with automatic diaphragm).

Hasselblad

Contaflex

Exakta

Viewing what you take through a ground glass places the reflex cameras in the class of the press and view cameras—except for small size and lack of distortion correction. View, compose, focus —all through the viewer.

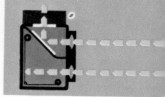
Twin-lens reflex has separate lenses for viewing and taking picture.

Twin-lens reflex cameras These have two lenses: one catches your picture, the other is for viewing. The image appears on a ground-glass screen, as in the single-lens type. Most take 2¼ x 2¼ in. pictures, so enlargement isn't the problem that it is with the 35 mm. Some have adapter backs; hence you can take color slides as with 35 mm. Lenses not interchangeable in most types, you can't use telephoto, portrait, or wide-angle lenses.

Advantages Good-size contact prints and fine enlargements possible. Ground-glass composing and focusing as on single-lens reflex, without mirror flip.

Disadvantages Parallax at close distances unless type with built-in correction; depth of field cannot be directly observed as in single-lens type. Lenses can't be changed in most models.

Agfa Optima Reflex

Yashica-Mat LM

Rolleiflex E2

Automatic J66 Land

Automatic 100 Land
with flash

Pathfinder 110B

POLAROID CAMERAS The big advantage of these cameras is that they develop their own pictures in the camera. Take your picture, wait ten seconds (50 seconds for color), strip out your finished picture. Polaroid cameras use 8-exposure Polaroid Land film, which works on totally different principles than conventional film. Because you are able to see how your picture comes out immediately after taking it, you can correct for mistakes. This is useful for checking your exposure on bounce flash and for learning how to use such equipment as filters. With some types of Polaroid Land film there is considerable control of contrast in the development of the film. You get but one print per shot, but copies or a negative can be secured by sending prints to the manufacturer.

HOW POLAROID LAND CAMERAS WORK

positive paper

reagent pod

negative paper

◄ Negative, in different chambers from positive, moves past lens and is exposed.

Exposed negative is pulled around roller, where it meets positive sheet. "Pod," containing chemicals, is broken when the two rollers press the sheets together. ►

Rollers spread reagent. Metallic silver deposited from negative forms image. ►

positive   negative

Stereo Realist

Kodak Stereo

Kodaslide Stereo Viewer

STEREO CAMERAS are 3-D cameras. Equipped with two lenses plus the viewer lens, they see as you do—with two eyes. Instead of one picture, you get two: one of what your left eye sees and one of what your right eye sees. These two pictures are slightly different. When you view these near-twin pictures through a special viewer, each of your eyes sees one of them, and the original scene appears in three dimensions. Seen through stereo hand viewers, the realism and depth of these 3-D pictures is superb.

SUBMINIATURE CAMERAS vary from one built into a cigarette lighter that sells for about $10 to one with speeds up to 1/1,000 sec. and all the basic devices of larger cameras, that sells for nearly $300. Most take 16 mm. film in black-and-white and in color. Transparencies are mounted in 2 X 2 frames so regular slide projectors are used. Most subminiatures have fixed focus like box cameras; some have focusing lenses of excellent quality.

Most subminis control light by shutter speed only. Their inconspicuous size (easily slipped into shirt pocket or purse), ease of operation, and low film cost have given the subminiatures a growing popularity.

Minolta 16-P
Subminiature

Mamiya Deluxe 16
Subminiature

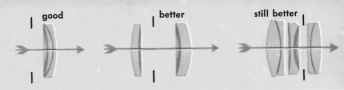

good   better   still better

ABOUT LENSES No camera is better than its lens. And the better the lens, the greater is its proportion of the total cost of the camera.

In a box camera the relatively simple lens is entirely adequate for the job it is asked to do. But it will never have the sharpness of a more complex lens. For more precise work—and for a wide variety of shots under different conditions—the design of lenses becomes very complicated. A single lens may be built up of four or five different pieces of glass—each specially made, ground, and polished with meticulous care.

The faster the lens, the larger it is in proportion to its focal length and the more difficult it is to avoid various types of distortion. So the job of producing a fine, fast lens is very exacting. The result costs money. In recent years the better lenses have been coated with a material which reduces surface reflections.

A fast lens has real advantages. But in stepping-up from an inexpensive to a better camera, remember that extreme lens speed, like car speed, is seldom necessary. For most of us it is a luxury.

Keep in mind the advantage of interchangeable lenses (available, with one exception, only on focal-plane or behind-the-lens shutter cameras). Wide-angle lenses are particularly useful in shooting interiors or when you want a wide-angle view from close up. Telephoto lenses are excellent for portraits (you can stand back and avoid distortion, yet get a close-up), as well as for nature work. So a camera on which lenses can be changed quickly has distinct advantages.

ABOUT SHUTTERS A shutter is a light gate, opening to admit light when an exposure is made. A good shutter will open fully in the shortest possible time and close again promptly. It must do this precisely at speeds of up to possibly 1/1000 sec. So another item of expense in a good camera is a shutter that will work reliably.

Lens-mounted shutter

Most shutters are spring-operated. Some are self-setting; when you press the button, this sets the spring tension and then trips the spring. Some cameras have shutters that must be cocked before each shot. When you advance the film, the shutter is automatically cocked. Or the cocking may be an entirely separate operation.

The usual lens-mounted shutter opens and closes on the center line of the lens. Quite different is the focal-plane shutter, which operates inside the back of the camera, just in front of the focal plane (plane of focus) of the lens. A focal-plane shutter is something like a tiny window shade with slits of various widths across the curtain. When you click the shutter, the curtain speeds across the face of the film and light passes through one of the slits. Setting the shutter for a certain speed moves the curtain along so that the slit of proper size for that speed will sweep across the film. The advantage is that it provides precisely the same amount of light for each part of the film. The lens-mounted shutter provides less light to the edges than to the center.

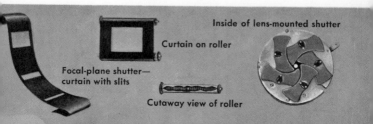

Inside of lens-mounted shutter

Curtain on roller

Focal-plane shutter—curtain with slits

Cutaway view of roller

GOOD PICTURES WITH ANY CAMERA A good camera is a fine tool, and in the hands of an expert it will give unexcelled pictures. But skill and perseverance with any camera pay dividends in excellent prints and transparencies. Here are some good shots, each made with a different type of camera.

World Wide, Inc.

◀ This human-interest story was recorded with a press camera.

This shot of a mother Robin providing a grasshopper meal for her hungry young was taken with a single-lens reflex camera. ▶

LaVern Frost—Popular Photography

◀ This study of a boy peering through a grating tells its story well. It's the low camera angle that made this box-camera picture outstanding.

This peaceful barnyard scene was made on Kodachrome Film. Lighting and composition were what took this picture out of the ordinary. ►

◄ Proper lighting brought life and texture to this woodland shot. Kodak Ektachrome Film was used. Note how light angle emphasized the grain of wood.

A good camera is important. But any type of camera will take good pictures if used with insight. Side lighting got this picture on Kodak Ektachrome Film. ►

CAMERA CARE A good camera deserves good treatment. Never try to lubricate or repair your camera yourself. Take it to a camera shop for routine, expert inspection yearly.

Do: Keep your camera in a case to protect it from dust, sand, bumps. Cases are inexpensive insurance against mishaps.

Do: Protect the lens from long exposure to bright sunlight which builds up heat and can ruin the lens permanently.

Don't: Let it get hot. Good lenses won't take it. Keep your camera out of the car's hot glove compartment. Don't let it stand in the sun for any period of time.

Do: Keep your lens clean—spots show on film. Use approved lens tissue and cleaner. Wipe with gentle, circular motion.

Do: Clean dust from inside of camera once or twice a season. Use a soft brush made for the purpose.

Do: Keep it in a place that is dry to avoid mildew.

Darkroom Magic

There's a touch of magic to darkroom operations. A blank film becomes a negative. White printing paper reveals a beautiful picture right before your eyes. But there's more than magic to this. When you develop and print your own pictures, you can correct for defects in the original shot, bringing out what you want and subduing other less important parts. Thus you can make pictures really your own. This book has stressed many things to do before the shutter clicked. There are many more things to do after it clicks. Developing, printing, and enlarging all help you to do a better job of making your pictures just what you want them to be.

105

3 trays

developing solutions

safelight or bulb

FIXING BATH

STOP BATH

DEVELOPER

graduate

viscose sponge

print frame   thermometer   No. 2 printing paper   2 film clips

BASIC DARKROOM EQUIPMENT Five or ten dollars will cover the basic materials for developing. Don't invest more until you've given the darkroom a try. Start with one of the ready-made beginner's kits or purchase the things you need separately. The list below will carry you through to finished prints. Later on, when you have gained control of your materials and want to experiment further, add a good enlarger and gadgets that make darkroom work easier, faster, better, and more fun.

Here's All You Need To Get Started

3 trays (8 x 10 in.)
1 viscose sponge
1 orange safelight or bulb
1 pkg. #2 printing paper
1 print frame or a contact
  printer
1 thermometer
1 32-oz. graduate

6 packages of developer mixes
1 package of hypo
2 film clips
2 print tongs
2 glass stirring rods
1 daylight developing tank
1 bottle of stop solution
  (acetic acid)

WHERE TO WORK   You can begin in any room or space which can be temporarily darkened. Kitchens or bathrooms are best. A sink and running water are almost essential. But the one absolute requirement is complete darkness. Work at night, or make a wood or heavy cardboard inset that fits tightly into the window frame. Use masking tape around the edges. Two handles will make the job of inserting and removing it easier. Place towels or rags at bottom of door to avoid light leaks there.

A kitchen counter or table next to the sink, or a board cut to fit the top of the bathtub, will provide working space. You will need both a safelight and a regular light, so fix with separate switches. The arrangement of the apparatus should allow a smooth, convenient plan of work from printing frame to final washing. Table tops should be protected from spilled solutions by several layers of newspapers or a piece of oilcloth.

Running water, electrical outlets, sink and shelves make the kitchen about the most convenient place to work.

DEVELOPING COMES FIRST

Developing is the process of changing the latent film image to a visual one and fixing the negative so light won't affect it further. The film must be developed before you can make a print from it. Printing is more fun, so you may prefer to have your films developed commercially and then do the printing yourself.

Tank developing can be done with the lights on once the light-tight tank is loaded with film in total darkness. Tank development is easiest way to do film.

1 Loading film onto tank reel in complete darkness takes practice. So practice feeding already-developed film on reel. Don't touch the emulsion side. When you can do it in the dark without fumbling, you're ready to start. Lights out—complete darkness! Remove film from 35 mm. cartridge, or separate from backing if roll film. Load tank reel. Replace lid. The rest of your work is done with lights on.

2 Temperature of your developer, stop bath, and fixer should be lowered or raised to 68°F. in water bath. These chemicals can be bought ready to use or you can mix your own from powder form.

3 Pour developer into clean measuring glass. Use enough to cover film in tank. Pour this into tank. It goes through light-tight cover. Rinse measuring glass.

4 Agitate tank every 30 sec. or so. Keep tank in tray of 68°F. water when not agitating. Leave film in developer for exact time indicated on developer package (about 5 to 7 min.). Pour out developer through lid of tank.

5 Pour in stop bath (plain water will do). Purpose of the stop bath is to stop developer action quickly and to rinse it from film so fixer can work properly. Pour out stop bath.

6 Pour in fixer through hole in tank lid. Purpose of fixer, usually called hypo, is to remove undeveloped silver salts from film so that light will not affect film further. Leave film in fixing bath for time indicated on package, agitating tank every 30 sec. or so. Pour out fixer. Now your film will not be hurt by light.

7 Wash film in slowly running water for recommended time. One way to do this is to remove film from tank and place, in loose folds, in sink of cool water (about 68°F.). Leave a thin pencil of water running from tap. Another way is to leave film in tank, remove cover, and allow a thin stream of water to enter tank from rubber or plastic shower hose attached to faucet. The stream should be just enough to keep water circulating constantly in tank.

8 Dry film the following way: Fasten a film clip to each end, and hang film by one clip to hook or nail in wall or shelf. Hold other clip in left hand and pull down slightly to hold film taut. Wipe down both sides of film with a dry-damp cellulose sponge. Wipe down slowly in one firm but gentle stroke. Allow film to hang until completely dry. (Film should be developed and dried in as dust-free a place as possible.) Now your film is ready to print. Cut film to convenient lengths and store in glassine or paper envelopes that have been marked for easy identification.

LET'S LOOK AT YOUR NEG-ATIVES
Here's a perfect negative, exposed right and developed right. Bright, sharp highlights and good detail in important dark areas.

Do your negatives sometimes look like this? Generally too dark and with no detail in important shadows? Highlights muddy and indistinct? It was overexposed.

You probably have some negatives that look like this one. It was underexposed. The entire negative is thin and washed out. No detail can be seen; not enough contrast.

Got any like this one? Streaks, blotches, and stains mean bad darkroom technique. The film wasn't properly fixed or washed. Stick to directions and agitate film in processing.

These scratches came from careless use of tongs in developing tray or from careless handling of film. Keep fingers off emulsion until film is dry!

HERE'S HOW NEGATIVES TURN OUT Here's a perfect picture—because it was printed correctly from the perfect negative at top of opposite page.

This one is overexposed. The dark, muddy negative on opposite page produced a thin, washed-out print. However, corrective printing (p. 114-115) can make a better picture.

This one is underexposed. The thin, washed-out negative on opposite page produced this too-dense, dark picture. Again, corrective printing could correct for the negative defect.

Now look at this one. Not much can be done in printing to save this picture. You might as well destroy negatives that are stained and blotched.

See how the scratches show when a print is made from a scratched negative. **Tip:** A little Vaseline smeared on negative makes scratches less noticeable on print.

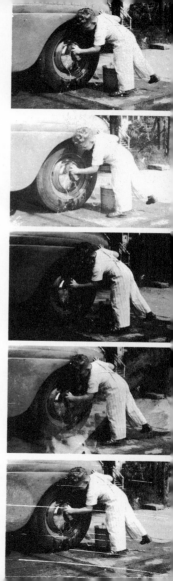

Printing frame and clamp are used to hold paper against glass during exposure.

Printing box has built-in light for exposing print.

PRINTING completely reverses the negative image. Light passes through your negative to reach the emulsion on the printing paper. Where the negative is black, no light gets through and the print comes out white. Where the negative is clear, your print will be black. The chemical process of printing is identical to that in developing a negative, but different developers and fixers may be used.

Use orange safelight three feet or more from your work space. You will need three trays: for developer, stop bath, and fixer. Printing paper is less sensitive than film. So prints can be developed in the open trays with safelight letting you see your print "coming up" in the developer. You also need a printing frame or box. The frame has spring clamps to hold film and paper tightly against the glass during exposure. The printing box is about the same, with a light inside. For printing frame exposures use a goose-neck lamp with a 40-watt bulb. Finally, you need printing paper. Start with No. 2, glossy paper for normal negatives.

1 With solutions all ready, and safelight on, select a negative, cut it from the roll, and place it, dull side (emulsion) up, in the printer or frame. Over it place a sheet of No. 2 printing paper, emulsion (shiny) side down (the emulsion of the film should face the emulsion of the paper). Clamp down back to hold paper and film together.

2 Place frame, glass side up, about 1 ft. beneath the lamp. Turn on the lamp for about 3 sec. Use same exposure for a printing box. Negatives vary, so you'll learn exposure best from experience.

3 Slip exposed paper into developing solution, shiny side up. Make sure it is all covered. Rock tray gently. In 15 to 20 sec. the darkest areas will appear. In a minute your picture should look right.

Now into stop bath for a few seconds (use tongs to move print).

Lift out with another pair of tongs and drain a few seconds. Now into fixing bath, face up. Rock tray periodically. After 3 or 4 min. inspect. Leave in fixer for 5 or 10 min., rocking occasionally.

4 Then wash—and wash! Keep a pencil-size stream of water running into the sink or pan, draining to keep fresh water coming in. Agitate prints every 10 min. or so. Wash for 1 hour or more. Some new chemicals shorten washing time.

5 Gently mop each print with wad of absorbent cotton. Place face down between blotters or in blotter roll. Leave for 2 hours or more.

CORRECTIVE PRINTING Here is where you can become creative after your photograph is taken. If you have a negative like picture 1—flat, thin, and underexposed—and you print on No. 2 paper, using normal exposure and developing time, it will look like picture 2. To get more contrast, use as little exposure time as possible in printing (1 to 3 sec.), but leave print in developer longer—perhaps 3 min. Stop before print starts to fog and whites turn gray. Then your print should look like picture 3. **Tip:** If print is slow in coming up, or if an area shows no detail, rub it lightly with a developer-wetted finger. Or better, much better, use a paper with more contrast (No. 3 or No. 4). Picture 4 was made from same negative, but with No. 4 paper at normal exposure and developing time. A negative like picture 5 (generally dark and with too

much contrast) gives a print with little tone gradation between the blacks and whites. The original exposure was too long. If you print on No. 2 paper, using normal exposure and developing time, it will look at best like picture 6. To correct, use No. 1 paper. It will cut down the contrast and minimize the blacks. Picture 7 was made from the same negative, using a No. 1 paper. If the blacks are still too strong, with everything else washed out, try No. 0 paper. Then your print should look like picture 8.

Remember to use No. 2 paper for normal negatives. Use 1 or 0 for high-contrast negatives, and 3, 4, or 5 for low-contrast or thin negatives. Varigam and other "variable contrast" papers come in one grade—special filters convert them to 10 grades of contrast. Use glossy papers for detail and brightness, rough papers for texture effects.

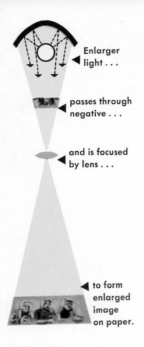

Enlarger light . . .

passes through negative . . .

and is focused by lens . . .

to form enlarged image on paper.

ENLARGING Of all dark-room processes, enlarging is the most fun—the most rewarding. The technical term for it, projection printing, tells the story, for the process is very like contact printing except for one detail. In contact printing the negative and the printing paper are in contact with each other. In enlarging the negative and printing paper are separated and light is projected through the negative to the printing paper below. As the light goes through the negative, it shoots out in an expanding cone. If the printing paper is placed close to the negative, a small enlargement will be made. The farther the paper is placed from the negative, the larger the image size and the resulting enlargement. Theoretically, one can enlarge without limit. A postage stamp size negative can be blown up to fill a screen as big as a house. But, practically, there are very real limits.

First, the negative must be sharp and clean-cut. Otherwise, magnification increases fuzziness and destroys whatever detail already exists.

Second, the grain of the film—the fineness or coarseness of the tiny silver deposits which make up the negative—also limits enlargements. Grain shows up most in areas of flat tone, as in sky or smooth water. If the grain is coarse, the enlargement looks mottled or freckled. Fine-grain films (such as Kodak Panatomic-X) should be used

116

when you plan big enlargements. Very fast films usually have coarse grain structure and seldom can stand enlargement of more than three or four times original size.

Third, remember that the greater the enlargement, the longer is the exposure required. The hot light sources in some enlargers tend to make the film buckle or blister. Once damaged, the film is useless. So the size of the enlargement is determined in part by the amount of time your film can stand your enlarger's heat.

Details stand out and the dramatic quality of small print is increased by enlargement. Defects, as well as details, are magnified, so select best negatives for good enlargements.

ABOUT ENLARGERS An enlarger opens up new photographic vistas. While it gives you large prints from small negatives, it also gives you something much more important—control. You can manipulate an enlargement, accenting some parts, holding back others, even adding or taking away parts of the picture. Contact printing offers little control. Enlarging offers much. So get an enlarger if you want professionally finished pictures and an additional creative approach to photography.

While an enlarger projects light and a camera does the reverse, both do so by means of a lens and should be thought of in the same terms. A good enlarger, like a good camera, is a precision instrument. If you have a good camera, buy a good enlarger. If your camera has the best of lenses, be sure your enlarger does too (or get one on which your camera lens will fit, if the lens is of the demountable type). In any event, get an enlarger of as good quality as your camera—or the one you expect to buy some day. When you buy an enlarger, you are making a lifetime investment. Take time to study the advantages and special features of various makes and get the one that best fits your needs.

There are three basic types of enlargers: those with a condenser lens between the light and the film; those with

Diffusion-type enlarger throws a soft light through negative.

Diffusion-condenser gives enlargements that are sharper.

Fluorescent - type enlarger diffuses light like diffusion type.

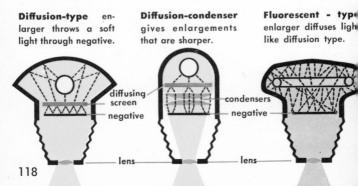

diffusing screen
negative
condensers
negative
lens
lens

Easel

Timer

Foot switch

a frosted diffusing light source; and the diffusion-condenser types which combine a condenser lens with a diffusing glass. The condenser type gives the sharpest enlargements, but it tends to magnify grain, scratches, defects, and even dust on the negative. The diffusion type is better for the average worker, but the prints may lack sharpness. Most widely used are the diffusion-condenser enlargers which provide satisfactory sharpness without objectionable magnification of film defects. One type of enlarger has a circular fluorescent light inside a specially designed reflector head.

In buying an enlarger, look for sturdiness, rigidity, lens quality, and ease of handling. Constant focusing and adjustment are required in enlarging prints. Check the adjustments and controls. Try the enlarger for sharpness and lack of distortion. Finally, get a large-size easel to hold your paper.

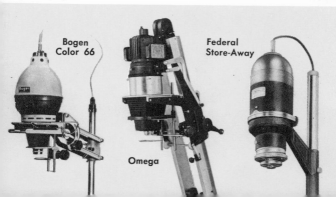

Bogen Color 66

Omega

Federal Store-Away

HOW TO ENLARGE Enlarging is similar to contact printing. Use the same solutions, with trays as large as your biggest enlargement. For first experiments, use 8x10 in. paper. Enlarging papers come in a variety of sizes and surface textures, single and double weight. Start with No. 2 grade, single weight, glossy or smooth. Later, try others. ("Variable contrast" papers come in a single grade; contrast is changed by use of special filters.) Use an orange safelight at 4 ft. Test for safety by covering half of a strip of enlarging paper with an opaque object and exposing for several minutes with safelight on. If uncovered portion of paper turns gray on developing, move farther away or use a smaller bulb.

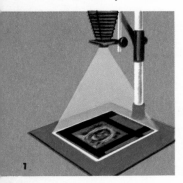

1 Select a good negative and place in negative carrier, emulsion (dull) side down. Place a sheet of ordinary white paper on easel. Turn safelight and enlarger light on; room lights off. Carefully focus the negative image (pick out some sharp line or detail) on the paper.

2 If the image is too small, raise the enlarger head and refocus. If too large, lower the head. When you're set for size and focus, turn off the enlarger light and put a piece of enlarging paper in place of the paper used in focusing.

3 To find out the best exposure time, cover all but ⅕ of the enlarging paper with cardboard. Turn on enlarger light. At the end of 5 sec. pull the card back another ⅕ without turning light off. Repeat process at 5-sec. intervals until the entire sheet is exposed—the last ⅕ for only 5 sec. Turn off your enlarging light. Slices of the paper have been exposed, in order, for 25, 20, 15, 10, and 5 sec. (After you get experience, use a narrow test strip of enlarging paper instead of entire piece.)

Place the test paper in the developer. In about 1 min. you'll be able to tell which section got the best exposure. If the full 25-sec. section is still too light, repeat the test process, starting at 25 sec.

4 Place fresh enlarging paper on easel and expose. Place exposed paper in developer, emulsion side up. Be sure it is completely in solution; use tongs to hold down. Rock tray gently. Leave print according to developer instructions, or until print looks good under safelight.

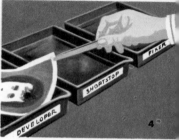

Place in the stop bath for a few seconds. Lift out and drain with hypo tongs and put into fixer. After 2 min. you can turn on the light. Leave print for time indicated on package, rocking tray occasionally. (Leave too long and you'll bleach print — too little and print will fade.)

5 Wash print for an hour in running water. **Tip:** Hypo is heavy and tends to settle to bottom. Let pencil-sized stream of water run into sink and use stopper with a small hole in it to allow hypo to drain out the bottom while water also runs off at the top drain hole in sink.

6 Wipe lightly with a damp sponge. Then place flat between photo blotters until fairly dry. Then place a book on the blotters for weight and let your print dry for a few hours or overnight.

121

Here's one way to do cropping. Cut out two cardboard "Ls." Print a picture, small size, of the entire negative; now arrange your "Ls" in different positions on the small print. Working in full light with a finished print, you can see precisely what you're getting. Now crop and enlarge just that part.

CROPPING FOR COMPOSITION

While enlarging, you can rearrange your picture for more emphasis or to get rid of distracting background. You can take a group picture and enlarge one person to make an excellent portrait. This simple process of cutting out unwanted portions is called cropping.

Here's how. There are two "Ls" on your enlarging easel. Turn on the enlarger light and throw the negative image on a white paper. Move the "Ls" in and out until you've selected just the part of the picture you want. To make it larger, raise the enlarger head. Now expose and print that portion of the negative.

Print lacks emphasis.

Better composition and a better picture result from intelligent cropping. ▶

Cropped print removes expanse of wall and focuses attention on subject. ▼

Diane Pattou

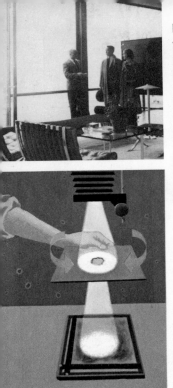

BURNING IN with light helps if you have a good negative some part of which is overexposed. Longer exposure in your enlarger would darken that part, but it would also cause all darker areas to lose detail or to go completely black.

To avoid this, cut a hole about the size of a half dollar in a large card. Expose the entire print in the enlarger light for the normal time, then hold the card over the paper. Move it up or down until the light coming through the hole covers an area slightly larger than the section you want to darken. Keep the card moving in small circular motions so that you won't get sharp shadow edges. After a few seconds (depending on how much darkening is required) turn off the enlarger light and develop the print as usual. Although this process is called burning in, it's really painting with light.

Note the picture at the top of the page. The background is almost completely white. The picture at the bottom of the page has been burned in, and the trees outside of the house now show. However, the figures near the window are too dark. This brings us to the problem of dodging.

DODGING is the opposite of burning in. Use it when you have a print in which an area is so dark that it has lost all detail.

When dodging small, well-defined areas, put a tuft of cotton or small disc of cardboard on the end of a stiff wire. As the exposure is being made, hold this utensil in the

Dodging disc in use

path of light so that it hides the too-dark area. Move it about briskly, in circular motions, to prevent the formation of a hard line of shadow. Develop as usual.

Paul Weller

Notice photographs on opposite page. Figures and furniture near window are too dark. Defects in original print have been corrected by burning in background and dodging foreground. To dodge an irregular area like this, you will need a piece of cardboard which conforms roughly to the shape of the area to be dodged. Get your focus set. Then place a card on a box in enlarger light path and trace the area to be dodged. Cut this out and use it for dodging.

125

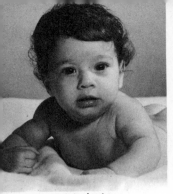

Original print

VIGNETTING Sometimes you want to get rid of the background entirely or to remove other objects from around your subject. Cropping will do it, of course, but there's another way that's called "vignetting." It gives an interesting portraiture touch to your print.

Cut a hole in a cardboard. The hole should be just large enough to form an area of light the general size and shape of the area you wish to vignette when you hold the card about halfway between the enlarger lens and the printing paper. Make the edges of the hole jagged and keep the card in constant circular motion to avoid sharp shadow edges. This will give you a gray-fading-to-white background.

Jagged edges in the hole of the card should look like this.

Vignetted print

126

Photograph distorts buildings.　　　　Enlarger corrects distortion.

DISTORTION CORRECTION Most types of cameras produce linear distortion when tilted to shoot tall buildings or other high places. If you have an enlarger, tilt the easel up until the image is corrected or, if your enlarger has a calibrated swivel, swing the head sideways until the vertical lines have straightened out. In either case, cut down your lens aperture. You need more depth of field, for one part of the print will be farther away than another. Focus at the center of the print—both top and bottom will be very slightly out of focus.

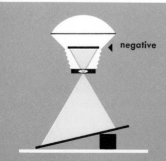

negative

Distortion correction with most enlargers is best done by tilting easel. Place negative in carrier and white paper on easel. Focus image. Raise edge of easel until distortion is corrected. Block in position and refocus center of image (both low and high edges of image will be slightly out of focus). Replace white paper with printing paper and expose in usual manner. If enlarger has swivel head, easel may be left flat and enlarger tilted.

Arrange articles, expose.

Develop print as usual.

Result is a photogram.

PHOTOGRAMS

No camera is used, but they're photographs just the same. Shadowgraphs is a better name, for they are actually negative shadows on printing paper.

They are simple to make. Using a safelight, put a sheet of photographic paper — contact or enlarging — on a flat surface. Arrange on it a composition of articles, preferably small things that have sharp outlines. Grains of sugar, wheat, dandelion umbrellas with their tiny seeds, tacks, kitchenware, leaves — the possibilities are endless. Then turn on a light above it for a few seconds, turn it off, remove the articles on the paper, and develop the print in the usual way. As you become more familiar with the process, you will be able to make quite intricate compositions.

The background should be deep black, the shadows white. Exposure, of course, will depend on the strength and distance of the light. Overexposure can't hurt, though sometimes you'll want a light shadow effect—then expose briefly. Set a small bulb at least 3 ft. above your paper for sharp photograms. Otherwise you'll get fuzzy edges.

GREETING CARDS Place cards, announcements, bookmarks, greeting cards—all can be made by photography. Any techniques can be used singly, or in combination — contact prints, photocopies, enlargements, photograms, model sets (the Nativity, for example), or abstractions. Work out your idea in simple form (first make a sketch). To print, fasten negatives and letters cut from black paper underneath

Arthur Lavine—Popular Photography

sheet of glass. Place printing paper under negative, expose under a gooseneck lamp, develop, and dry.

Production printing is your only real problem. Teamwork is the answer, with one person at the printer and the other developing. At the start, develop no more than 3 or 4 at once. Once you've found the correct exposure—expose 20 or 30, protecting the exposed paper from light until you're ready to develop.

You can make a card like this by using double exposure (see page 148).

PHOTOMURALS With negatives of minimum graininess and maximum sharpness, enlargements up to 16 x 20 in. or larger can be made and then combined to make effective photomurals or picture walls.

Take a series of pictures of the same scene (note the three pictures at top of page), swinging the tripod-mounted camera after each shot so that you cover new territory. But be sure each shot overlaps the one preceding. From the negatives make maximum-size enlargements. There are three ways in which you can make murals from these: 1. Mount separate prints on wallboard and run a molding strip between them. (Cut each picture so the effect is of a continuous print under the strips.) 2. Carefully tear the right side margin of each print, from front to back, in an irregular fashion and slide this into the proper position of the print to its right and glue firmly in place. The tear line shows on close inspection, but from a distance it looks fine. Bottom picture is a tear-mural. 3. Print each negative, in order, on a length of mural paper supplied in rolls. You'll need special troughs for developing and a helper to hold one end of the roll.

MONTAGES combine parts of several pictures to make a planned composition. Make a number of prints of the desired sizes, cut out their essential areas with a razor blade, and mount them on a common background. Make a copy negative of this (p. 146), develop, and print.

It is also possible to make a montage directly on a sheet of enlarging paper by successive exposures. Pencil the areas to be occupied by each picture on a sheet of paper by tracing the images, as projected by your enlarger. Next, make test enlargements to establish right exposures for uniform tone. Each negative will require a separate dodging card (p. 125). Put first negative in enlarger and focus on key sheet. Replace key sheet with enlarging paper. Hold dodging card in position and expose. Put printing paper in light-tight place, change negatives, and repeat the process until exposures are complete.

Separate photographs of the four common, everyday objects above were combined to make the unusual montage below. Objects were taken against white background, thus no dodging was necessary.

Paul Weller

131

A DARKROOM OF YOUR OWN is a great convenience. The more you use the kitchen or bathroom, the more you will appreciate the need for a conveniently arranged permanent darkroom in which to work.

Location of the darkroom will partially be determined by available space. Consideration should also be given to uniformity of temperature and dryness. Naturally, choose an area which can be made completely dark. The smaller the space, the greater the need for some sort of ventilation. If water is readily available nearby, you can get along; but running water in the room is preferable. Fix up a long drain board on either side of the sink to prepare solutions, to process both negatives and prints, and to carry on the long washings (a deep tray with a siphon is better for washing prints than a sink).

Have several electrical outlets for safelights, a printer, an enlarger, and at least one white ceiling light with a pull chain and a long cord stretched overhead across the room. Then you can have light by merely reaching up in the dark wherever you are.

You'll need a table for a contact printer and enlarger placed close to the sink board. Above it should be shelves for printing paper. Also useful is a work table, complete with cutting board, for finishing operations. There should be shelves for reference books, chemicals, film clips, a timer, and other equipment. Solutions should be kept in bottles under or beside the sink. Put a towel rack near the sink. Paper towels are best, because once tossed into a wastebasket, there is no danger of contaminating your fingers the next time you dry your hands. Have a place for a rubber apron or a smock to protect your clothing from damaging chemicals.

Keep your darkroom clean and orderly. Clean up after each session, for the dust of dried chemicals can be damaging to both film and paper.

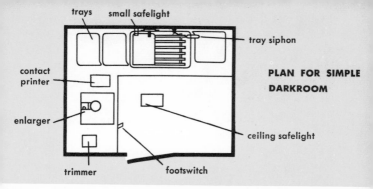

trays   small safelight

tray siphon

contact printer

PLAN FOR SIMPLE DARKROOM

enlarger

ceiling safelight

trimmer

footswitch

The simple darkroom above can be easily and quickly built by a carpenter or yourself, if you are reasonably handy with tools. A dry basement is usually the ideal location.

Size, equipment, and arrangement will vary with needs of individual, but preferably space should not be smaller than 5 by 6 ft. nor larger than 10 by 12 ft.

Muslin-covered wooden frames for drying prints slide in and out like a drawer and are under the bench to the right of the sink. Vertical compartments for tray storage are to the left. Counters should be covered with waxed linoleum that runs part way up the wall to protect it from splashed chemicals. Note adequate shelf space above working area. The counter height in the photograph below is 36 in., and the shelf height is 60 in.

35 mm. in strips for filing

Separate albums for prints

C-2

Number prints on back and file negatives in numbered envelopes.

CARE OF NEGATIVES AND PRINTS

As you accumulate negatives and prints, don't let them pile up. Negatives get scratched and prints dog-eared. Neatness pays big dividends in better pictures.

Throw away poor negatives. File your good ones in protecting envelopes, preferably glassine. Don't leave 35 mm. negatives in a roll. They may stick, always curl, and you can never find what you want. Cut into strips and place in envelopes. Identify each envelope. A loose-leaf notebook, with marked envelopes pasted shingle-fashion, makes an excellent file. Number each print to correspond to the envelope holding its negative. Place prints in vertical files or use separate albums for each general subject. Store transparencies in files designed for that purpose. Keep all materials in a dust-free, dry, and reasonably cool place.

Loose-leaf notebook makes convenient file for negatives.

File designed to hold transparencies.

Special Problems

Equipped with a telephoto lens, a modern camera can catch birds on the wing. With a bellows attachment or close-up rings, it can snap insects or other tiny objects, which can then be enlarged. With a microscope your camera can probe the invisible world; with a telescope, the moon and the planets. Even a box camera can be used for many special pictures. So here is a section about special pictures and special techniques. For ones which require the use of a darkroom see pp. 128-131.

Hummingbird flight was stopped by 1/3000-sec. strobe flash.

NATURE PHOTOGRAPHY Nature photography provides all the thrills of hunting, and more. The chief problem is to get close enough for rewarding shots. For birds or squirrels a simple solution is to set up a feeding station outside a window. After birds begin coming regularly, fasten a 6-in. board to one end of the feeding station. Place food at the end of the board. Put a dark cloth over the window. Cut a hole through it for the camera viewer and lens. With camera steadied on a tripod or table, focus on the food pile. Keep your eye glued to the viewer and shoot whenever a bird hops into view. Birds move quickly, so use the highest shutter speed possible under existing light—never less than 1/50 sec.

Another solution calls for remote control. Use a long shutter-release cord (10 ft. or more), which can be purchased from any large photographic dealer. Fasten your camera securely near a bird's nest, water-hole, or other place where wildlife may appear. Camouflage the camera with a piece of burlap—and wait.

For best results make a blind out of a light wooden

Camera clamp

Close-up kit

frame covered with burlap or a small tent. Camouflage with grass, leaves, or branches. Leave the blind for several days, till wildlife get used to it. If it is portable, gradually move it forward toward what you want to photograph. Use a telephoto lens whenever possible.

Get photographs of turtles, frogs, and snakes from captured specimens. Put the subject in a refrigerator (not deep freeze) for a half hour before photographing. Cold makes the animal sluggish and easier to handle. Try photographing these animals on glass with illumination from below and above. Photographing birds on the wing requires shutter speeds of 1/100 sec. and preferably faster; an electronic flash is a real help at close range.

Nature photography requires a knowledge of plants and animals as well as of your camera. As you get more experience with both, your pictures will improve.

Bee on clover, f/8 at 1/10 sec.   Gulls in flight, 1/200 at f/8

STAR PICTURES Star pictures can be made with any camera, though starlight is too dim for anything but time exposures unless you use a telescope. Try making star trails on your film—streaks of light which show apparent star movement resulting from the earth's rotation. Use fast film and a tripod; set up the camera pointing toward the North Star. Focus at infinity, with the lens wide open. Use an exposure of at least 2 hours to get interesting results. (Be sure to place the camera where street or house lights won't fog the film.) As the earth turns, each star makes a light streak on the film; the longer the exposure, the longer the streak.

Northern Lights are dim at best. You'll need a time exposure (experiment with it), with the camera on a rigid tripod. Include foreground detail at the horizon. Experiment with color film as well as black and white.

Star trails exposed 3 hours at f/8, average-speed pan.

Northern lights exposed 20 sec at f/6.3, average-speed pan.

Solar eclipse. Exposures 5 min. apart at f/22 and 1/100 sec.

ECLIPSE PICTURES of sun or moon are most interesting when you take a series of shots at exactly timed intervals on one negative. The whole story of the eclipse is then told on one picture.

Basic procedure is the same for sun or moon, but exposure problem is different. For eclipses of the sun, use a deep red filter (Wratten A or darker), your smallest aperture, and your highest speed. Protect eyes when looking at the sun or aiming the camera. Look through over-exposed film unless sighting through a single-lens reflex with red filter. For shots of the moon, no filter is needed. Expose at about 1/10 sec. at f/5.6.

For any eclipse, place your camera on a tripod or block it rigidly. Set it up so that the first shot will register near the margin of your film. Successive exposures will march across to the other side. With camera rock steady, open shutter at exact intervals—every 5, 10, or 15 min.— depending on the size of your camera and the number of stages you want to show. Time exposure can't be used as earth's spin will cause streaks. Foreground detail adds perspective.

Yerkes Observatory Photograph

Total eclipse of sun through telescope with 15-sec. exposure. Bright area is corona.

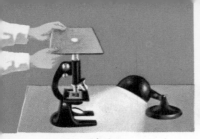
Focusing with tissue paper

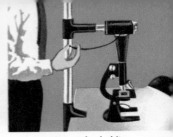
Attachment for holding camera

SHOOTING WITH MICROSCOPE

Scientific photomicrography generally requires a single-lens reflex camera, or 35 mm. cameras with special attachments for direct focusing. But even simple cameras will do. Focus the microscope carefully on a brightly lighted specimen. Move a piece of tissue paper up and down above the eyepiece to discover the point where the light circle is smallest and sharpest. Clamp the camera solidly (or use a sturdy tripod) so that the front of the lens is precisely at this point. Open the diaphragm; focus at infinity. Use black paper to form a light-proof collar connecting 'scope eyepiece and camera lens. Experiment with exposure—usually 1 to 5 sec. Use cable shutter release. With a single-lens reflex you can see what you're shooting and take living specimens, but it's tricky since strong illumination is required for shots at 1/50 sec. or less.

Pollen magnified 140 times.

Microphotograph of Water Tige
Roman Vishniac

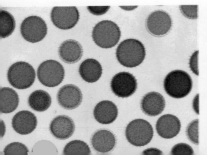

Front view   Side view

CAMERA AND TELESCOPE Shooting through a telescope or through binoculars is much like photomicrography. Your success depends more on quality of 'scope
and brightness of object than on camera lens. Choose
clear, still nights. First try the moon (craters and mountains
show best when moon is not full). Load camera with
Kodak Tri-X Film or other fast film and place on
tripod. Prepare a black paper collar, made for simple
and jar-free attachment, to connect the camera lens with
the low-power eyepiece of the 'scope. With single-lens
reflex, connect lens and eyepiece—gently—and focus
through ground glass. With other cameras use tissue paper (see p. 140) to determine precise place for setting
front of camera lens. For a quarter moon, 1/5 sec. is
about right. More than 1/2 sec. will cause blur, due to
earth's rotation. To photograph sun, see p. 139.

Moon's craters taken through a filter with a 40-in. refractor.

Yerkes Observatory Photograph

New York's Battery shot at f/16 and 1/200 on Kodak Plus-X Pan.

AERIAL PHOTOGRAPHY Take your camera along on your next air trip. Even if the day is clear, use a haze filter (no increase in exposure needed) for color or for black-and-white shots. Look for dominant landmarks and contrasting land patterns that will add interest to your picture. A portion of the plane's wing in the foreground will give increased depth. Focus at infinity; use shutter speeds of 1/100 sec. or better, or vibrations will blur your picture. Hold camera tightly and keep arms from touching plane. Clean window first and place lens close to it but not touching it. Shoot at an angle that minimizes reflections. For best shots of the ground, shoot when the sunlight is slanting across it, making shadows that give texture and depth. When flying near the ground, shoot back or ahead at the highest shutter speed possible.

Aerial shot catches geometric pattern of contoured farmland.

Scene shot on pan film.   Same scene with infra-red film.

INFRA-RED PHOTOGRAPHY   Infra-red rays are heat rays. You can't see them, but they can make a picture on special infra-red film. Pictures have even been made by the heat of a hot flatiron. Scenics made with infra-red film and a deep red filter give dramatically different black and white colors. Skies appear black, green grass and trees, white.

A chief advantage of infra-red photography is that it pictures far-distant objects that are invisible to your eyes and ordinary film because of haze. Compare the pictures at the top and bottom of this page and notice the penetration of haze by the infra-red film. Infra-red film is sold in sheets and in 35 mm. size only. If you use infra-red, try a few shots with infra-red flash lamps in complete darkness. There'll be no visible light, but you'll get your picture.

Haze obscures distant mountains.   Infra-red film cuts through haze.

EXTREME CLOSE-UPS

Anything pictured at 3 ft. or less is a close-up. Auxiliary lenses for box and other simple cameras enable these to focus down to 3 ft. Such lenses are excellent for portraits, but some cameras can be used to get extreme close-ups (hyper-close-ups or photomacrographs). Then you get precise and accurate focusing down to 6 in. or less.

About life size

Hyper-close-ups open up a new world. Small objects, or parts of them, are photographed life-size or larger. Enlargements turn your subject into an object of incredible interest, for such enlargements are of giant size compared to what the eye normally sees. The results are sometimes astounding. A small insect becomes a glowering monster. Even a dandelion becomes an object of geometric beauty.

Bigger than life

Hyper-close-ups are done with extension tubes or bellows which move the lens farther from the film, increasing the magnification. Basically, it is as simple as that.

Giant size

H. E. Berry—Popular Photography

Single-lens reflex and view cameras are ideal for hyperclose-up photography, for they pose no parallax problem. Look at the image through the ground glass; add rings or extend bellows until you get the magnification you want; compose, focus, and shoot. With other cameras, the camera lens and view-finder lens are apart, and cannot possibly converge on a close-up object. You can buy special gadgets for some cameras to correct for parallax. With others, you have to measure and guess.

The closer you get to your subject, the shallower the depth of field. To increase depth of field, use a small lens aperture and a longer exposure. This creates a problem when you are shooting living specimens. Place insects in your refrigerator until they are quiet. Keep flowers fresh the same way. Work quickly with animals. Use a twig, leaf, or rock to imply scale or habitat.

Experiment with exposure and try side lighting for three-dimensional effect.

Caterpillar

Grasshopper

Snail

Strawberries

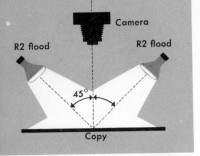

R2 flood Camera R2 flood

45°

Copy

PHOTOCOPYING To copy a picture or document you need two photofloods in reflectors, a drawing board or easel, and a firm tripod. With a view, press, or single-lens reflex camera you view exactly what you get. But any camera will do. Use a close-up lens if necessary.

Mount copy flat with thumbtacks or tape at center of board. Aim camera squarely at the copy; make sure front of camera is parallel with board to avoid distortion. Focus your camera carefully.

Set photofloods on either side of camera, at about a 45° angle to the center of copy, and each at the same distance from it. Look at copy from camera's point of view. Copy must be fully and evenly lighted. Shift lights until reflections are gone. If shooting copy under glass, use Polaroid filter to cut glare.

In copying line drawings and prints, develop your film for maximum contrast. Use a slow pan film and give it full development. Photographs or black-and-white pictures are best copied with fine-grain panchromatic film. Underdevelop slightly to keep contrast down. Use fine-grain pan film for color pictures, and correct for redness of photofloods with yellow-green filter on camera.

If your copy has considerable texture, as a painting with bold brush strokes or a piece of fabric with a rough surface, break the symmetry of your lighting by moving one light a little closer. Use a meter or, assuming two No. 2 photofloods at 4 ft. and a moderate film speed, try 1/5 at f/16, 1/10 at f/16, or 1/25 at f/8 and choose the best negative that results.

SCALE-MODEL PHOTOGRAPHY

Arrange your own sets and lighting to create dramatic pictures and the illusion of reality. Camera angle is important. Start with camera level or aiming up from beneath. Avoid anything that will destroy the illusion of realness—anything not in scale with the model itself. Hang model planes on fine, neutral-tone thread against the sky. Use gray cardboard for neutral backgrounds. Focus exactly and control depth of field to give background detail as needed. Arrange lighting for natural effect.

Note this ski jump picture. It was made from a 4-in. model, some wire, and cotton.

These seemingly lofty, multicolored pinnacles are only 4 ft. high. The photographer clipped a picture of a Ford automobile, backed it with cardboard, and put it against this setting.

Earl Smith

MULTIPLE EXPOSURES are a combination of several images on a single negative. Often useful, as in eclipse pictures (p. 139), they can also be used for amusing effects or for fantasy pictures.

You can create a group with a single person, for example. Select a setting with a uniformly dark background and no detail, as a dark drape or cloth. First, pose your model well to the left and expose. Without changing film or camera position, move subject to right half of scene and make a second shot. If you mark first position carefully by placing light chalk on the floor, you can move your subject for the second picture so precisely he can be shaking hands with or lighting the cigarette of the "first" person. You can make three or more shots on one film if you are careful not to let the subject's positions overlap—and so destroy the illusion.

You can use overlaps to create ghost pictures. This time, use background details. The second shot will make the subject appear transparent. Underexpose slightly for more ghostlike appearance.

A trick shot   A multiple exposure

TRICK PHOTOGRAPHY Create amusing trick effects by taking advantage of the fact that objects at a distance appear smaller than when close up. A boy at a distance will be smaller, for example, than a nearby bottle. To make the picture at the left you will need two negatives. Slip a sheet of black paper inside a bottle and photograph it on a table, with your camera at close range and on a tripod. Then take a picture of the boy against a black background. Your camera will need to be at a greater distance, so that the body of the boy occupies the same space on the negative as does the bottle. Sandwich the two negatives together in the enlarger and print them.

The photograph below is a combination of three different pictures. The prints of the man and of the apple were pasted on the print of the archer and background. A single shot was then made of the composite photograph.

Sun-dappled swimming pool on Kodachrome, 1/50 at f/5.6.

ABSTRACT DESIGNS Many modern artists are interested in the abstraction of subject matter—that is, they concentrate on the essential form of a subject and not on its lifelike reproduction. Abstract photography can be equally interesting. The only limits are those of your own imagination and resourcefulness. Try the sun-dappled water of a pool, smoke swirls, unstopped action, or complicated patterns of light and shadow. To photograph a

pendulum's motion, set camera on floor. Cover flashlight lens with black paper through which a small hole is punched. Hang flashlight by a string 4 ft. above lens. Focus; set shutter at Time. Turn off room lights. Give flashlight gentle push; open shutter. Leave till light comes almost to rest.

Pendulum tracery. Ten-min. time exposure period.

Home Movies

Movie making is no more difficult than still photography. The simpler cameras have a fixed focus, just like box cameras. The shutter speed is about 1/30 sec. Set the aperture at f/16 and you can take good pictures under all average conditions. For Kodachrome Film f/8 is about standard.

Movie making should begin where still pictures leave off. A good still picture can imply motion, show its direction, and suggest what may happen a second or two later. A good home movie should go beyond this—tell a complete story with the action interestingly portrayed through a series of closely knit scenes.

Anyone can take good motion pictures in black and white or in color with modern cameras and films. As in still photography, the difference between good pictures and outstanding pictures lies in knowing what to shoot, how to compose your subject, and how to take advantage of the lighting and best camera angles. There is one additional problem—and opportunity. Movies show motion. What action to select and how to arrange it in the best sequence is the crux of home movie making.

SHOOTING HOME MOVIES

Work from a script.

Hold camera steady.

Get a story in mind. Your movie should tell where, when, what, and who. Use a simple written script and jot down all sequences you want to take before shooting.

Hold camera steady. There's nothing worse than a scene that jumps over the screen. Some use a tripod. It's particularly important when you're following close action moving in and out of your field of view.

You don't have to take scenes in the sequence you will show them. Shoot in the most convenient order, but get all scenes necessary to set locale and tell your story. Rearrange for best story by editing, cutting, and splicing.

Lighting is much the same as in still photography. Avoid excessive contrast and scenes that alternate in brilliance. Flat lighting, with the sun behind you or slightly to one side is best for most outdoor movies—particularly color. Use No. 2 floods and exposure meter for indoor work. Check with meter when you change from long shots to closer ones.

Panoramic shots cover scenes too broad for single-position shots. But

Edit later.

Front lighting is best.

don't overdo panning. Pan smoothly and slowly to a point of interest and hold there for a second or two.

Average shots should last about 6 sec.—none shorter than 2 sec. or more than 12. Remember that by splicing and editing you can bring together the four seasons of the year.

Long shots establish locale—give the setting for the action to follow. Also use long shots to introduce new action. Try high- and low-angle shots for special effect.

Use medium shots—10 to 12 ft.—to show the bulk of the action, but change back and forth to accent the story. Make your changes smoothly.

Use close-ups for emphasis; to point out detail; to show exactly what is happening; to catch an expression. Watch how commercial movies use angle shots and change position.

Closing up on your subject while the camera is running provides drama and interest. It's easy with a zoom lens. Just "zoom in" from where you stand. With ordinary lens, use tripod on a dolly made of boards mounted on caster wheels. Move up slowly, changing focus as necessary.

Long shots show locale.

Medium shots for action

Close-ups for emphasis

Tripod for steadiness

Bolex Supreme

Bell and Howell 310
with Zoom Lens

Kodak
Automatic 8

Radiant
Colormaster

Superpod

MOVIE EQUIPMENT No need to spend a large amount of money to enjoy home movies. You can buy all you'll need for as little as $100. Start with an inexpensive camera.

Essentials A camera, projector, and screen are all you need. Home movie film comes in 8 mm. and 16 mm. The 8 mm. cameras and film are cheapest and use a 3-ft.-wide screen; 16 mm. is larger, favored by semi-pros. Projectors are more expensive than cameras of the same quality.

Useful accessories Telephoto and wide angle lenses increase the versatility of your camera. Or use a camera with a zoom lens. Or buy a turret model which holds three lenses. Almost a necessity is a firm tripod with adjustable head. An exposure meter will help. Finally, you'll find a film titler and film editor great conveniences.

Kodak Automatic 8
Projector

Kalart Editor Viewer

BOOKS TO READ

Photography as an art and a science encompasses such a wide field that literally hundreds of books have been written about it. Of the many that are suitable for beginners, here are a few that may help you with your next steps.

Deschin, Jacob. *Say It with Your Camera: An Approach to Creative Photography. Second Edition.* Ziff-Davis, 1960. An excellent book for the accomplished amateur.

Eastman Kodak Company. *Kodak Reference Handbook.* New Edition, 2 volumes. Eastman Kodak Company, Rochester, New York, 1954. Excellent technical and other reference data for the serious photographer. Loose bound to permit adding or upgrading individual Kodak Data Books.

Feininger, Andreas. *Successful Color Photography.* Third Edition. Prentice-Hall, 1957. An elementary but complete introduction to color, color film, and color photography for the serious amateur.

Miller, Thomas H., and Brummitt, Wyatt. *This is Photography: Its Means and Ends. Garden City,* 1959. A well-illustrated, readable introduction to black-and-white and color photography. One of the best.

Neblette, Carroll B., *Photography—Its Materials and Processes,* Van Nostrand, Princeton, New Jersey, 1962. For those who are interested in photography as a profession as well as a hobby, this contains practical information on lenses, lighting, modern color processes, color reproduction and presents latest theories and advances.

Sussman, A.: *The Amateur Photographer's Handbook,* Thos. Y. Crowell, New York, rev. 1962. Basic handbook dealing with all phases of photography.

In addition to these, there are many books on specific phases of picture taking and making—reflex photography, miniature photography, sport photography, portraits, photographic optics, photography as a business, and many others. Consult reference libraries and your photographic dealer for more information. Also make use of the excellent photographic magazines: *Popular Photography,* *Modern Photography, U.S. Camera,* and others. Finally, do not fail to take advantage of the books and pamphlets published by the various film and photographic companies. These include general guides to photography and detailed bulletins on specific techniques or types of apparatus.

PHOTO CREDITS

Any interested person can become a better-than-average photographer. One of the best ways to do this is by joining one of the thousands of photography clubs in this country. Make inquiry at the photo store, museum, or school for a camera club in your vicinity.

INDEX

A